Coffee with the Pastor

Colossians: Living in a New Reality

MIKE HILSON

CONTENTS

ACKNOWLEDGMENTS

I want to thank my wife, Tina, who has been my partner in life and ministry: I love you! To our three boys, Robert, Stephen, and Joshua, thank you for taking this journey of ministry with us and having a great attitude about it along the way. Also, thank you for growing up to be reliable, solid men I can count on and in whom I take great (hopefully godly) pride.

I want to sincerely thank my family at New Life Church for giving me the freedom to grow as a leader and follower of Christ.

Most importantly, I want to thank and praise God!

ABOUT THIS BOOK

People sometimes ask why I would take the time to write a book. The answer is really quite simple and two-fold. First of all, I want to be able to speak with my children, grandchildren, and great-grandchildren about this wonderful gospel I have been given the honor of working for all my life. I want them to see the joy and power of living a life guided and protected by God's Word, God's Spirit, and God's commands. In doing so, I hope to establish many generations of my family in the wonderful grace of our Lord.

So I write as a father.

I also write as a pastor.

New Life Wesleyan Church has become a rather large body of believers meeting in multiple services and multiple locations across multiple states. While all of that is a huge praise report and blessing, it creates its own set of challenges. It has become impossible for me to sit down individually with folks in the church and have deeper conversations about the power of God's Word and how it can be applied in their lives. And so this is the reason for a series of books called *Coffee with the Pastor*.

As I write these books, I do so with a great

deal of care and caution. They will read, to many people, like a commentary of sorts. However, let me warn you about that thinking. I am not qualified to write commentaries. I am not a theologian. I am not a scholar. I am simply a pastor. It is my job to help as many people as possible read and better understand the Word of God. His Word is powerful and life changing. If you can just get into it and understand what it is saying, then you can see the God of Heaven through the blood of Jesus and the power of the Holy Spirit. That will change your life! Therefore, though this work is bathed in as good as an understanding of theology as I can attain, the goal is not theological. The goal is practical application of life-changing, biblical truth.

That is the purpose of this series of books. That actually is the purpose of my ministry, and it is the ultimate goal of my life.

So grab a cup of coffee, understand that I am no scholar, open up your Bible, and let's get you thinking about what God can do in your life!

INTRODUCTION

Freedom and Holiness

These are the overarching themes of Colossians. As the apostle Paul writes to the believers in Colossae, he does so realizing they are facing two massive forces that both threaten the long-term stability and viability of their faith.

On the one hand is the ever-lingering presence of the Jewish legalism. These Judaizers insisted that the Gentiles who converted to Christianity adhere to Old Testament laws of lifestyle. They demanded that every non-Israelite functionally become an Israelite in order to be a Christian. To those who were confused, challenged, or discouraged by this teaching, the apostle writes clearly: *"Since you died with Christ to the elemental spiritual forces of this world, why, as though you still belonged to the world, do you submit to its rules: 'Do not handle! Do not taste! Do not touch!'?"* (Colossians 2:20-21). To those who are struggling with the rules of this world, the apostle presents freedom.

There were other philosophical and religious forces of the day that were unconcerned with righteous living and, in fact, very comfortable with blatant sinfulness and immorality. To them, the apostle writes just as clearly: *"Put to death, therefore, whatever belongs to your earthly nature: sexual immorality, impurity, lust, evil desires and greed, which is idolatry"* (Colossians 3:5). To those who were trapped in lifestyle choices that were damaging to their faith, relationships, and health, the apostle clearly presses forward the very real possibility of holiness. *"Therefore, as God's chosen people, holy and dearly loved, clothe yourselves with compassion, kindness, humility, gentleness and patience. Bear with each other and forgive one another if any of you has a grievance against someone. Forgive as the Lord forgave you. And over all these virtues put on love, which binds them all together in perfect unity"* (Colossians 3:12-14).

So here in Colossians, the apostle Paul once again demonstrates to us the intricate, often difficult, and yet Spirit empowered art of balance.

Since Christ set you free … be free!

Since Christ is holy … be holy!

"After this letter has been read to you, see that it is also read in the church" (Colossians 4:16).

WEEK 1

Day 1

"Paul, an apostle of Christ Jesus by the will of God, and Timothy our brother, To God's holy people in Colossae, the faithful brothers and sisters in Christ: Grace and peace to you from God our Father. We always thank God, the Father of our Lord Jesus Christ, when we pray for you, because we have heard of your faith in Christ Jesus and of the love you have for all God's people—the faith and love that spring from the hope stored up for you in heaven and about which you have already heard in the true message of the gospel that has come to you." (Colossians 1:1-6)

Grace and peace. It always starts there.

Grace for the forgiveness of our sins brings peace as we finally live in the presence and wholeness of our God, our Creator, our Father, our Savior, our Sustainer.

Grace and peace. It always starts there.

But it doesn't end there.

Far too often, Christians accept the grace and forgiveness of God through Jesus, and then they simply sit down and wait. They wait for Jesus to return, for the Holy Spirit to do something, or for God to take us all home in a rapture event. We just find grace and sit down. It seems to me that this is not what God intended when He sent His son Jesus as a sacrifice for us. When the Holy Spirit came and filled us as God's

1

chosen people, He did not do so in order to help us sit more comfortably. There is much for us to do. There is much for us to change. There is much to do and change within us. There is much to do and change within our culture. We should not simply get saved and sit. We should find salvation and get to work!

In this letter written by the apostle Paul to the church in a town called Colossae, he begins by commending them for their *"faith in Christ Jesus"* and *"love … for all God's people."* These two attributes are central to a proper reaction to grace and peace. Many would simply choose to get saved and then settle in, but that just isn't enough. Jesus warned about such thinking when He gave the parable about a foolish, rich man (Luke 12:13-21). It seems that this man had been greatly blessed with a bumper crop (God had shown great grace). He therefore did not need to worry about providing for himself or his family; they had plenty (God had given peace). His reaction is the problem. *"Then he said, 'This is what I'll do. I will tear down my barns and build bigger ones, and there I will store my surplus grain. And I'll say to myself, "You have plenty of grain laid up for many years. Take life easy; eat, drink and be merry." ' "* (Luke 12:18-19). This is the way many Christians seem to react upon finding grace and peace: "I have found grace that forgives my sins. I have found peace knowing that my eternity is all stored up and reserved for me in heaven. So I'll say to myself, 'You have eternal hope and reward, take it easy, pray, hang out at church, and be happy!' "

The problem here is we forget Jesus' reaction to this man: *"But God said to him, 'You fool!* [When God calls you a fool, it's getting serious!] *This very night your life will be demanded from you. Then who will get what you have prepared for yourself?'* " (Luke 12:20). When we take the approach of this foolish, rich man in our lives, we risk having the same reaction from God: "You foolish Christian! You have no idea how long you have on this earth! When you are gone, where will your peace be and what good will it be to those you did not tell?" When we get saved and settle in for a long, slow, comfortable slide into the arms of our waiting Savior, we fail to change. We are actually repeating the same sinful patterns we had before. We have just spiritualized them. We are living for ourselves and resting on our salvation. Essentially, we are refusing to show concern or offer help to the world around us. We are refusing to be renewed, redeemed, or re-made in the image of the One who left the throne of heaven to suffer and die for us. He did not give His life so that we could just sit and rest. He wants us to be changed and re-made. In turn, we could lead others to Him, which would ultimately change and re-make the culture around us.

The Holy Spirit lives in us so that we might

truly learn to have a life-changing *"faith in Christ Jesus"* and culture-changing love for God's people. Instead, we tend to remain committed to our own carnal, selfish comforts. We will love God's people as long as they don't try and change our style of music or change our building. We will love them as long as they don't bring "those" people in and ruin our quiet atmosphere. We will love them as long as they don't cause us to feel uncomfortable because "those" people are not like us. We will be committed to changing the world as long as we don't have to do anything uncomfortable or difficult. Just have the world become like us. Have them find their own way in, and they can have all the same grace and peace we have.

If any other follower of Christ should ask us to do or sacrifice something that is difficult to do or let go … it's on!

That is not what God has called us to; we are called to live by, *"the faith and love that spring from the hope stored up for you in heaven and about which you have already heard about in the true message of the gospel."* That call demands that we *"make disciples of all nations"* (Matthew 28:19); we become *"witnesses in Jerusalem, and in all Judea and Samaria, and to the ends of the earth"* (Acts 1:8); we offer our *"bodies as a living sacrifice, holy and pleasing to God"* (Romans 12:1); we rid ourselves *"of all malice and all deceit, hypocrisy, envy, and slander of every kind"* (1 Peter 2:1) ... and the list could go on and on! The grace and peace we find in Christ must never be used as an excuse to just sit and settle. It must be used as a springboard and encouragement to go and serve!

It is true; heaven awaits us! How many will we take with us on the way?

Day 2

"In the same way, the gospel is bearing fruit and growing throughout the whole world—just as it has been doing among you since the day you heard it and truly understood God's grace. You learned it from Epaphras, our dear fellow servant, who is a faithful minister of Christ on our behalf, and who also told us of your love in the Spirit. For this reason, since the day we heard about you, we have not stopped praying for you." (Colossians 1:6-9)

Three things I would like for us to take a look at here.

Feed the Movement

The gospel, or good news of Jesus Christ, has been expanding and reaching people since the day it was first preached by Peter in Acts, chapter two, on the day of Pentecost. We should keep in mind that the apostle Paul was likely in Jerusalem on the day of Pentecost. While he was not a believer at the time, he undoubtedly saw the powerful display of the Holy Spirit. (Paul converted to Christianity in Acts, chapter nine, after a life-altering encounter with the risen Christ on the road to Damascus.) He experienced the virtually overwhelming reaction of the people as they flocked into the ranks of this new religion. Paul, or Saul as he was known prior to his conversion, would have been alarmed that so many were led into following this Jesus person who he saw as a fake.

Then Saul met Jesus ... and that changed everything.

That really is the secret of the gospel. Jesus changes everything. The good news is that, in Jesus, we can find forgiveness for everything we have ever done wrong. There is no depth of sin from which Jesus will not forgive and deliver. Then there is the work of the Holy Spirit. While Jesus offers us forgiveness, the Holy Spirit offers us power. Jesus forgives us of sin and the Holy Spirit empowers us against returning to sin. These two, forgiveness and power to change, work together to bring hope that the world cannot simply offer. The world only offers conditional surrender to sin. They offer methods and philosophies designed to either excuse sin or manage sin.

"Don't drink too much."

"A little lie is not so bad."

"Everyone else is doing it, so go ahead and have some fun."

"What difference does marriage make as long as you love each other?"

Jesus and the Holy Spirit actually offer forgiveness and freedom from sin. This is a truth that everyone needs to hear! The words of the apostle written 2,000 years ago are still true today: *"The Gospel is bearing fruit and growing throughout the whole world—just as it has been doing among you since the day you heard it and truly understood God's grace."*

Our work, our calling, our command from God is to feed this movement of the gospel of peace and freedom. Everyone needs this. There is not a single person in the world that does not need forgiveness for something or freedom from something. Jesus offers both! We must be about the business of feeding the movement and growth of the good news of Jesus Christ!

Connect the Faithful

There is another truth here. *"You learned it from Epaphras, our dear fellow servant, who is a faithful minister of Christ on our behalf, and who also told us of your love in the Spirit."* We should constantly be about the work of Epaphras. We should not only spread the good news of Jesus' forgiveness and the Holy Spirit's power but also connect believers together. Far too often, we think we are in this fight alone. "I am the only Christian at my workplace. My church is the only believing church around. Our family is the only Christian household in our neighborhood." These statements are rarely true. The truth is that God has His people everywhere. Even in countries where Christianity is illegal, there are Christians who work, live, and secretly worship the God of Heaven. They may be under threat, but they are there. If Christians exist in the most dangerous places on the planet, they are certainly at your workplace, in your neighborhood, and in other churches. For us to somehow believe we are the only ones left, is a thought based either in ignorance or arrogance. Ignorance can only be dealt with through information, learning, and telling the stories of those who follow Christ around the globe. Arrogance can only be dealt with through repentance. If you are somehow convinced that you, your group, or your church are the only true believers in your community, city, or town, then may I be direct with you?

You are being a jerk!

To dismiss every other group or church in your area that calls on the name of Christ is just wrong. Other churches may not worship the same way we do or even carry the same doctrines. If they are preaching the Word of God and doing all they can to bring people to the saving grace of the blood of Jesus, quit fighting the family! Those who lead others to the redemptive sacrifice of Jesus are our family. They are not the enemy. Trust me, we have enough real enemies without fighting each other! I heard an old evangelist once say, "If I walk into town and find an old, mangy, half-dead dog in the middle of the road, but that dog is barking the name of Jesus, I'll support him!" I tend to agree. We need to put far less effort in fighting each other and far more effort in connecting those who are barking the name of Jesus!

Pray for the Saints

Once we have identified those who are working to claim the name of Jesus, we should pray for them, constantly. The apostle Paul often repeats this thought in different words in his letters: *"We have not stopped praying for you."* Those who will follow Christ will face difficulty. The enemy of God and our souls, the Devil, will not leave us alone. He is intent on destroying the work of Christ, and the only way we can wage war on him is through prayer. When we see others doing all they know to serve and live for Christ, we should pray for them constantly. We should pray without stopping and without excuses. I have often spent hours inside of the church I pastor walking around the sanctuary. Many of those who attend regularly tend to sit in the same general area each week. I see them. Even when I don't get to speak to them, I see them. So when I am walking the sanctuary, I will, at times, intentionally look around the room. As I look into that area where they sit, I will pray for them. I will ask God to empower them, embolden them, protect them, encourage them, and use them. I have done this all throughout my ministry. While it has become more difficult and less effective as the church has grown and as we hold many services now, I still try from time to time. The point is that whatever it takes, however you can remember to get it done, and as often as you possibly can, pray for the saints. Pray for the pastors. Pray for the believers.

Pray ... and do not stop praying!

Day 3

"We continually ask God to fill you with the knowledge of his will through all the wisdom and understanding that the Spirit gives, so that you may live a life worthy of the Lord and please him in every way." (Colossians 1:9-10)

There are a number of great calls the apostle gives to us in these verses. Let's take a look at three of them.

Finding Understanding

The apostle implores us again and again to keep praying. He is very specific in this verse as to what he is praying about. He does not begin his prayer for the Christians of Colossae by asking for blessing or strength. He begins by asking for understanding. As a pastor, I am often approached by those seeking wisdom in some great, or not so great, decision in their lives. They want to seek and find God's will, and they hope that somehow I can enlighten them on that will. The truth is that I am just another human slogging through this sin-sick world and wrestling with my own understanding, or lack thereof, of God's will and plan. While it may be true that I have spent more time contemplating God's Word and how it can and should affect the lives of His people, I am no prophet. So I will often answer such a moment by pointing people toward prayer. It is the Holy Spirit that actually gives understanding. Enlightenment comes from God, not the pastor. While God may choose to speak a helpful word through a pastor, friend, or stranger, catching truth, understanding truth, and applying truth is the work of the Holy Spirit in your life. Surround yourself with the Word, worship, and people of God, and you will eventually hear the voice of God. When that moment comes, you will come to know and understand the will of God.

Developing Wisdom

The early church struggled against a theology known as Gnosticism. This theology, which the apostle Paul battles against in many of his letters, claims to have found some depth of knowledge that cleanses and sets free those who have come to possess it. They believed that they were set free by their knowledge. However, Christ says we are set free by His blood given to us through His grace and accessed by our faith. Smarts are not required! In fact, this understanding that the apostle is praying for is not an understanding that leads to salvation. Salvation is already present! J. Vernon McGee speaks to this when he suggests that, "Instead of praying, 'We ask this of Thee,' the prayer should be, 'We thank Thee for all that You have already done' " (McGee 1983, 337). So we are not praying for a wisdom or knowledge that saves; we are praying for an understanding that guides. Again, McGee gives a clear interpretation when he translates this phrase as: " 'I pray that you might be filled with knowledge, that you might have superknowledge.' But Paul confines this knowledge to knowledge of the will of God" (McGee 1983, 337). What we are seeking is not knowledge that makes us smarter than everyone else. In fact, we are not seeking knowledge that is even about anyone else. We are seeking knowledge about ourselves. How should I think? How should I understand? Where am I going? How should I live?

Living Worthy

That understanding must then be applied. There is an old saying that I use a lot: "Jesus loves you just as you are … but He loves you too much to leave you just as you are." Our faith should change the way we live. As one commentary says it, "The end of all knowledge, the apostle would say, is conduct" (Spence and Exell 1950, 5). Our knowledge, even our intelligence, is useless if not properly applied. Knowledge that is not applied in life is merely trivia. Trivia doesn't change the life of the holder of the trivia. It can mislead the holder of the trivia into thinking that he or she actually holds wisdom. When all that is held is trivial data that does little to expand the thinking of a trivial life.

However, when one actually applies knowledge in proper and effective ways to daily life, one attains wisdom. Wisdom is the goal. Wisdom allows us to live above the sin that once held us down. Wisdom from the Holy Spirit can actually allow us to *"live a life worthy of the Lord."* And if we can live a life worthy of the Lord, then we can *"please Him in every way."* This is the goal for a multitude of reasons. First and foremost, we owe Him. It is Jesus, the Son of God, who gave His life for our sins. He gave up the splendor of heaven and the throne of the universe. He came to be the image of God and the sacrifice for sin that we could not find on our own. Jesus shows us God, and Jesus opens the door of grace for us. We simply owe Him our very best, but there is more. A life lived in the wisdom and knowledge of the Holy Spirit is a life lived well. When we follow Him, we avoid all the pitfalls of the enemy. We avoid the damage of sin and the devastation of failure. A life surrendered to the understanding that is gained from the Holy Spirit is a life that we will enjoy living. It is a life that will make a positive difference in the world around us.

Day 4

"Bearing fruit in every good work, growing in the knowledge of God, being strengthened with all power according to his glorious might so that you may have great endurance and patience, and giving joyful thanks to the Father, who has qualified you to share in the inheritance of his holy people in the kingdom of light. For he has rescued us from the dominion of darkness and brought us into the kingdom of the Son he loves, in whom we have redemption, the forgiveness of sins." (Colossians 1:10-14)

Now let's take a look at three more calls to holiness we find here in chapter one.

Be Productive

When we gain understanding and knowledge from the Holy Spirit and apply it to how we live, our lives begin to be productive. We can bear *"fruit in every good work"* not because we are smart or talented, but because He is guiding our every move. It is true that a person can be productive without following the guidance and goodness of the Holy Spirit. That kind of productivity produces something dramatically different. While the world can train us and enable us to produce worldly good, the Spirit enables us to produce spiritual or eternal good. This spiritual good is not to be confused with some mystical or ethereal good that is never easy to see or understand. On the contrary, these good works are "beneficial, practically good" (Spence and Exell 1950, p. 5). It can sometimes seem that we as Christians are playing word games with the notion that we need to do good works in this world. We will assign value to mystical things. Then we somehow think that those immeasurable, intangible things we have produced relieve us from the requirement of making a physical and practical change in the world, but they don't. It is true that through prayer, petition, worship, and discipleship, we see great strides and progress in the spiritual realm. However, we are also called to make a measurable, tangible difference in society. No manner of spiritual change can replace the physical change that is so desperately needed in our world. We must strive for growth and change in both worlds. We must bear *"fruit in every good work"* as well as bear fruit in every good way.

Be Strong

Hopefully you are tracking with the progressive nature of these words. We pray so that we can find understanding, live worthy, and be productive. This is the path of discipleship. This is the path of spiritual growth that leads to practical change. If we are to see this process through, we must be strong and endure. As Christians, we are constantly swimming against the tide. Society is drawing us away from Christ and holiness, not toward them. The enemy of our souls, the Devil, is constantly attempting to divert our attention and change our direction. Endurance is required. Endurance requires strength. That strength comes from the Holy Spirit. The apostle makes praying for strength and endurance part of his prayer for us as believers. He does not pray that we would be delivered **from** our struggles or our culture. He instead prays that we would be delivered **through** our struggles and our culture. The difference between the two is stark. If we are delivered from our struggles, we miss out on the opportunity to develop the spiritual muscle of strength that increases our capacity and value to the Kingdom of God. If we are delivered from our culture, we are deprived of the opportunity to affect our culture for the cause of the Kingdom of God. We need these struggles. We need to be engaged in our culture.

It is true that both our weaknesses and culture work to separate us from our Savior. As they work to do so, we can remember the words from the apostle Paul in another letter he wrote to the church in Rome:

> *Who shall separate us from the love of Christ? Shall trouble or hardship or persecution or famine or nakedness or danger or sword?... No, in all these things we are more than conquerors through him who loved us. For I*

am convinced that neither death nor life, neither angels nor demons, neither the present nor the future, nor any powers, neither height nor depth, nor anything else in all creation, will be able to separate us from the love of God that is in Christ Jesus our Lord. (Romans 8:35-39)

Give Thanks

Once again, watch the progression. We pray so that we can find understanding, live worthy, be productive, be strong, and for all of this we should give thanks! Gratefulness to God is one of the great missing components of the Western Church in my opinion. We have for far too long demanded of God. "Make me whole! Make me wealthy! Make me smart! Make me a winner! Make me well! Make me happy!" None of this is what God promised us. None of this is even the point. Our prayers, though we strive mightily to pray them in as humble a way as we possibly can, are often little more than demands of God. We constantly remind Him of what we think He should be doing. We constantly demand that He fulfill what we think we need. When all the while, He has given us His Son as a sacrifice for our sins and His Spirit to sustain us along our way. Even if we are not happy, through the Spirit, we have joy. Even if we are not whole, through the Spirit, we have hope. Even if we are not wealthy, through the blood of Christ, we have a mansion in heaven. Even if we are not well, through His grace, we have eternity waiting for us where there is no sin, no sorrow, no sickness, and no death! The only plausible response to this kind of grace ... is gratitude.

Day 5

"The Son is the image of the invisible God, the firstborn over all creation. For in him all things were created: things in heaven and on earth, visible and invisible, whether thrones or powers or rulers or authorities; all things have been created through him and for him. He is before all things, and in him all things hold together. And he is the head of the body, the church; he is the beginning and the firstborn from among the dead, so that in everything he might have the supremacy. For God was pleased to have all his fullness dwell in him." (Colossians 1:15-19)

"We now approach the real subject of the apostle's letter, and that which is its distinction and glory among the Epistles ... the Person of Christ" (Spence and Exell 1950, 7). Here the apostle Paul begins to unwrap for us a proper understanding of the person of Jesus.

Jesus is the Image of God

"The Son is the image of the invisible God."

One of the truly unique facets of Christianity is the fact that God makes Himself known to His creation. God reveals Himself to us in creation: *"For since the creation of the world God's invisible qualities—his eternal power and divine nature—have been clearly seen"* (Romans 1:20). He reveals Himself to us through His Word: *"Then the*

LORD said to Moses, 'Write this on a scroll as something to be remembered' " (Exodus 17:14). He reveals Himself to us through His Spirit: *"God has revealed to us by his Spirit. The Spirit searches all things, even the deep things of God"* (1 Corinthians 2:10). God ultimately reveals Himself to us through Jesus. In these verses, the apostle Paul is explaining that Jesus is the *"image of the invisible God"* or God in the flesh. This image is not to be taken as an imitation of God. That would be the best we could do as faulty humans. Jesus is the very person of God in the flesh so that we can see God, know God, and better understand God.

The apostle Paul is doing a very important work here for the Colossians. It is a work that is necessary with us as well. Colossian philosophy had completely separated the physical from the spiritual, making the assumption that the two never crossed paths or collided. In his description of Jesus, the apostle is breaking that barrier. They "assumed an absolute separation between the infinite God and the finite, material world, which was viewed as the work of lower and more or less evil powers" (Spence and Exell 1950, 8). Jesus broke down that wall of separation. Now God has come to man. The spiritual has invaded the physical. It has proven its dominance and love for the inhabitants of the "lower" existence.

Jesus means that God is truly with us!

Jesus is the Creator

"For in him all things were created."

The apostle then goes a step further. Jesus is the Creator. He agrees with the apostle John who opens his Gospel with the absolute declaration that Jesus is God: *"Through him all things were made; without him nothing was made that has been made"* (John 1:3). This Jesus who came to us, born of a virgin in a stable, raised in the house of a carpenter, baptized by John the Baptist, taught the multitudes about the Kingdom of God, performed miracles, died on a cross, and rose from the grave … this Jesus is the Creator God of the universe.

God is truly with us!

Jesus is the Ruler

"Whether thrones or powers or rulers or authorities."

There is no power that Jesus has not allowed. Rulers and authorities are either set up by God or allowed by God. One of the names for Jesus is King of kings. Meaning that there is no authority above Jesus. Just as God the Father, God the Son, and God the Spirit reign over the universe and everything in it, the God of Heaven rules over the entire earth as well. Kings and authorities ultimately answer to Him.

Again, realize what the apostle is saying. The God of Heaven has invaded the lower realms of earth and has come not to destroy but to redeem. He is not just the maker and ruler of the heavenly realms; His authority overrides all human authority. The God who made us loves us, and He is ultimately in control!

God is truly with us!

Jesus is the Sustainer

"He is before all things, and in him all things hold together."

When it feels like the world is falling apart, remember this: The God who made us loves us, is in control, and holds all things together! That means that those moments when we feel like everything is falling apart, things are actually falling into place! There is an old phrase among preachers and it goes like this: "I don't know what tomorrow holds, but I know **who** holds tomorrow!" I love that phrase. It rests on verses like this one. All I can do is watch the world fall apart, but Jesus can guide the falling pieces to the exact, right spot. As our plans fall apart, His plan falls into place.

God is truly with us!

Jesus is the Head of the Church

"And he is the head of the body, the church."

When my oldest son was very young, he would

come to church with his mother and me and watch as we did our pastoral work. One day, he looked at me and declared, "Dad you own the church!" I quickly had to put his young mind back in place. "No, son, no human owns the church. God owns the church. I just work for Him." My son made a classic mistake that is repeated constantly within churches. There is the assumption that the pastor is the owner, and in some cases the pastor does legally own the property (not in my case, to be clear). However, the church cannot be owned by anyone other than Jesus. God the Father clearly named Jesus as the head of the body, the Church. We all just work for Him. My role is like that of the head maintenance person at a great stadium. I hold the keys, fix things, expand things, replace things, clean things, and maybe manage a large team of paid staff. I am not the owner. The owner sits in a box seat in which I have no place in. I belong here on the ground floor taking care of everything the owner owns. I work at it, but He owns it. I find great peace in knowing that He is ultimately the head of the Church. He is far better suited for that job than me or any other pastor I have ever met!

God is truly with us!

Jesus is the First and the Last

"He is the beginning and the firstborn from among the dead, so

that in everything he might have the supremacy."

From beginning to end, Jesus is supreme. He was there when the earth was born, and He is the first one to have defeated death itself. Therefore, He is present and in charge of everything that exists between the beginning and the end. No matter where I sit in the timeline of human history, Jesus has supremacy. That means that He is in charge. So let's go through it again. The God who made us loves us and is in control from the beginning to the very end.

God is truly with us!

Jesus is the Fullness of God
"For God was pleased to have all his fullness dwell in him."

All of the fullness of God the Father dwells in Jesus the Son. For this reason, the following statements are all true:

Jesus' presence on this planet is stunning; God is truly with us.

Jesus' teaching of His Kingdom is profound; God is truly with us.

Jesus' authority over all things demonstrated in His miracles throughout the Gospels is humbling; God is truly with us.

Jesus' death on the cross paid the price for all sin over all time; God is truly with us.

Jesus' resurrection from the grave offers hope of eternal life to anyone who will receive Him; God is truly with us.

The divine invaded the natural. The eternal invaded the temporary. The majestic invaded the mundane. God is truly with us!

Day 6

"And through him to reconcile to himself all things, whether things on earth or things in heaven, by making peace through his blood, shed on the cross. Once you were alienated from God and were enemies in your minds because of your evil behavior. But now he has reconciled you by Christ's physical body through death to present you holy in his sight, without blemish and free from accusation—if you continue in your faith, established and firm, and do not move from the hope held out in the gospel. This is the gospel that you heard and that has been proclaimed to every creature under heaven, and of which I, Paul, have become a servant." (Colossians 1:20-23)

"So the LORD God banished him [Adam and Eve] *from the Garden of Eden to work the ground from which he had been taken."* (Genesis 3:23)

This is a really sad verse. Adam and Eve occupied a place of absolute perfection. The Garden of Eden was perfectly designed for their existence. God planned it for them and built it for them. Adam participated in naming all the creatures that leaped from the creative mind of an all-powerful God.

Everything they needed was there.

No sin. No sorrow. No sickness. No death.

Then they messed it up.

They did the one thing God told them not to do and were therefore banished from the Garden. From that moment to this one, God has been working to restore the broken relationship between God and humanity. In the Old Testament, this was accomplished through sacrificial worship. A sacrifice of produce from the ground or livestock from the herds was brought to the temple and given to God as a peace offering for forgiveness and praise. However, that system was limited, messy, and ultimately outdated. In reality, this system was put in place in order to teach mankind that sin was dangerous and damaging to the human condition. It required death to pay the price for forgiveness. Blood had to be spilled in order for sin to be forgiven.

Sacrifice had to be made.

Then enters Jesus!

Through Jesus, God would *"reconcile to himself all things, whether things on earth or things in heaven, by making peace through his blood, shed on the cross."*

Jesus, in one sacrifice, paid the debt of all sin.

No more animal sacrifice. No more bloody rituals.

Jesus paid it all.

I think that in today's world, we have really

lost sight of the ugliness of sin. Perhaps there was an advantage to carrying the very best, little lamb from your flock to the priest only to watch that priest slaughter it right in front of you. At least then you would vividly realize the deadly consequences of your sin. Today, sin seems somehow less dirty, less costly, and less deadly. Our culture has actually gone to great lengths to present sin as the fun in life.

My son and I recently attended a professional football game. It was so cold that we left early. On our way back to our car, we came across a young lady whom we had seen on our way into the stadium. When we passed her going into the stadium, my son said to me, "She's already lit!" He meant that she was very drunk and the game had not even started yet. Now, as we exited, there she was again. As we passed her, she fell face down onto the sidewalk. We stopped and helped her up. Then her slightly less drunk friend tried to help her along. They both ended up falling into some shrubbery, and so we helped them up again. Then finally other friends who seemed sober walked them to their car. As we were walking away, I was struck by how completely vulnerable that girl was at that moment. She set out that night to have a little fun. She ended up in a condition in which she would be entirely unable to defend herself from any danger. Sin left her unprotected from physical, emotional, and spiritual harm. Her sin could literally end up being deadly. I prayed a lot for her that night.

We don't have to live that way.

The blood of Jesus has paid the price for all sin. He paid the price knowing that somehow we would lose sight of how important the price. Perhaps this young lady had been told not to drink heavily. Perhaps she knew it was wrong, but she chose to do it anyway and that choice left her in a dangerous situation. In fact, her actions, like ours, left her *"alienated from God ... because of your evil behavior."* We all end up here at some point due to some choice we have made that separates us from God.

We don't have to live that way.

Jesus has *"reconciled you by Christ's physical body through death to present you holy in his sight, without blemish and free from accusation."* In other words, Jesus forgives you of your poor choices (sin) that alienate you from God. He already paid the price of your sin through His death. You can be *"free from accusation"* because Jesus (who is God) paid a price in His blood (sacrifice) for your poor choices (sin) so that you can be forgiven (reconciled). That is good news ... and there's more!

We don't have to live that way ... ever again!

Through the sacrifice of Jesus, we find forgiveness. Through the power of the Holy Spirit, we find a new life. It is through the Holy Spirit that we can continue in our *"faith, established and firm, and do not move from the hope held out in the gospel."* I hope you are catching all of this, because what the apostle is telling us is revolutionary!

We can be forgiven AND set free!

We can live differently AND better!

We can stand established AND firm!

We can find hope AND not be moved away from that hope!

While the world offers self-help and self-centeredness, Jesus offers forgiveness and hope.

God is truly with us … Jesus died for us …

We don't have to live in sin anymore!

Day 7

"Now I rejoice in what I am suffering for you, and I fill up in my flesh what is still lacking in regard to Christ's afflictions, for the sake of his body, which is the church. I have become its servant by the commission God gave me to present to you the word of God in its fullness—the mystery that has been kept hidden for ages and generations, but is now disclosed to the Lord's people. To them God has chosen to make known among the Gentiles the glorious riches of this mystery, which is Christ in you, the hope of glory. He is the one we proclaim, admonishing and teaching everyone with all wisdom, so that we may present everyone fully mature in Christ. To this end I strenuously contend with all the energy Christ so powerfully works in me." (Colossians 1:24-29)

As we discussed at the beginning of this chapter, we are not saved so that we can just sit. We are redeemed by the sacrifice of Christ so that we can engage the world around us through the ministry of the good news (gospel) of Jesus. Since we have found forgiveness and a new life, we should help others find that same forgiveness and new life. The work of helping others find Christ is called ministry. All Christians are engaged, or should be, in full-time ministry. A few make it a career, but all of us should be engaged in ministry. With that said, ministry is not without its difficulties. It also is not without its rewards. Let's take a look.

True Ministry is Truly Difficult

"Now I rejoice in what I am suffering for you, and I fill up in my flesh what is still lacking in regard to Christ's afflictions, for the sake of his body, which is the church. I have become its servant by the commission God gave me to present to you the word of God in its fullness."

Some seem to think that ministry should be easy and painless. Those folks are quickly disappointed. Ministry is difficult and costly. While we expect people to recognize that we are attempting to offer them the pathway to forgiveness and freedom, they often do not. When they don't understand what we are offering, things can get messy. The apostle Paul is in the middle of experiencing some of that messiness as he writes this letter to the Colossians. He is writing from a Roman prison. His declaration of faith in Christ Jesus has angered so many that he has now been imprisoned in Rome and is awaiting trial. From that prison cell, he writes four different letters: Ephesians, Philippians, Philemon, and Colossians. His imprisonment teaches us something profound about ministry.

The Minister is Suffering

From prison, the apostle Paul is suffering for the cause of Christ. Opposition and hardship have marked his ministry. He has been arrested, beaten, mistreated, lied about, driven out of town, threatened, and mocked. All of this, he has endured and yet has not given up. Why?

The answer is really quite simple, and Jesus states it to us: *"If the world hates you, keep in mind that it hated me first.... 'A servant is not greater than his master.' If they persecuted me, they will persecute you also.... They will treat you this way because of my name, for they do not know the one who sent me"* (John 15:18, 20-21). The world around us does not know the God we serve. If we expect them to act as if they do, we are not being reasonable or rational. The gospel is an offense to the world. The gospel of Jesus points out the sinfulness that the world has been trying to deny or hide. It calls them to repentance or submission to the authority of the Word of God and the Lord of lords. It calls them to stop what they love doing and serve what they currently hate, the body of Christ, the Church. All of that is going to bring about a negative, and sometimes violent, reaction from some in the world. We should just expect that.

Furthermore, ministry is difficult because the folks who are already part of the body of Christ are not always kind. They, too, can be offended by the suggestion that they are being callous toward the lost-ness of the world around them. They can be offended at the suggestion that their legalism is turning people away, or their lack of biblical center is offering people little more than a nice group of folks to do life with. When you challenge the traditions of some churches, you should be prepared for an all-out war!

So there are times when the minister is taking incoming fire from both sides. Ministry, whether volunteer or career, is difficult!

The Minister is Growing

Even in the difficulties and attacks from all sides, the minister is learning to lean on the everlasting and never-failing arms of Christ! In our difficulties, the Holy Spirit comforts, strengthens, and guides. Time and again, we will see people fail us. Time and again, we will see Christ sustain us! In those times of difficulty, we are learning and growing.

The Minister is Serving

No matter where you are or what circumstances you are facing, remember we are called to serve. The apostle Paul could have easily sat down in that cell in Rome and said, "Well, God let me be placed in prison, so I guess I have some time off!" He could have done nothing but just wait to be released. Instead, he wrote letters. He found a way to teach and spread the gospel of Christ even from the restrictions of a prison cell. He refused to give up in that cell, and because of that we have a wonderful epistle to teach us about the Christ who saved us!

No matter what your circumstances, there is a way to keep serving. Look for it. Seek it out. When you find it, work at it with everything you have. God's work and His Word will never fail to produce results, even if we can't see past our own prison bars!

True Ministry is Christ-Centered

"The mystery that has been kept hidden for ages and generations, but is now disclosed to the Lord's people. To them God has chosen to make known among the Gentiles the glorious riches of this mystery, which is Christ in you, the hope of glory. He is the one we proclaim, admonishing and teaching everyone with all wisdom, so that we may present everyone fully mature in Christ."

In the end, we only preach one thing — the teaching, crucifixion, and resurrection of Jesus who is the Christ! If we are teaching anything else, we are failing to remain true to our call. The truth is that Christ is what the world needs! Honestly, the world does not need another group meeting or cool self-help idea. The world needs the supernatural power of the Creator God of Heaven intervening on behalf of our broken and weakened state of reality. That is the message of Jesus! We need to unapologetically and confidently proclaim the truth of the forgiveness that can be found in Christ Jesus.

In trouble? Preach Jesus!

In prison? Preach Jesus!

Getting shot at from both sides? Preach Jesus!

No matter what ... preach Jesus!

"To this end I strenuously contend with all the energy Christ so powerfully works in me."

WEEK 2

Day 1

"I want you to know how hard I am contending for you and for those at Laodicea, and for all who have not met me personally. My goal is that they may be encouraged in heart and united in love, so that they may have the full riches of complete understanding, in order that they may know the mystery of God, namely, Christ, in whom are hidden all the treasures of wisdom and knowledge."
(Colossians 2:1-3)

J. Vernon McGee gives us a simple way to look at the content in chapter two: "In the first fifteen verses of this chapter we will see that Christ is the answer to philosophy. The remainder of the chapter will show that He is the answer to ritual. The answer to philosophy is for the head; the answer to ritual is for the heart" (McGee 1983, 347).

The apostle begins this section to the believers at Colossae by reminding them how much he cares for them. He is *"contending"* for them and for the folks at Laodicea. Colossae and Laodicea are two ancient cities that are very close to one another. While we learn of Colossae here in the apostle's letter, we learn of Laodicea in the writing of the apostle John. While banished to the isle of Patmos, the apostle John receives a vision from God that we know as the book of Revelation. In chapter one, the apostle John is instructed by *"someone like a son of man"* (this is the resurrected and glorified Jesus) to write down what he sees (Revelation 1:13). In chapter three, Jesus refers to *"the angel of the church in Laodicea"* and gives this warning: *"These are the words of the Amen, the faithful and true witness, the ruler of God's creation. I know your deeds, that you are neither cold nor hot. I wish you were either one or the other! So, because you are lukewarm—neither hot nor cold—I am about to spit you out of my mouth"* (Revelation 3:14-16). The Lord continues on and describes them as believing they are rich, but in reality they are poor. He then encourages them to *"buy from me gold refined in the fire, so you can become rich"* (Revelation 3:18).

The problem here in Laodicea, and likely in Colossae as well, is that the church was filled with people who believed they had accomplished much in their lives. They had wealth and comfort by the world's standards, yet they were still seeking Christ and a relationship with God. The problem was they didn't want to give up what they called success in order to take hold of what God called valuable. Many of them had never met the apostle Paul. Either the apostle had never visited, or they came to know Christ after the apostle's time there. Therefore, this infant church was facing the temptation to weaken and water down the gospel in order to maintain the worldly, familiar comforts and practices. They wanted to know Jesus, but not enough to actually change the way they lived. They wanted to be Christians, but they didn't want to be different. So the natural result was a church that was *"neither hot nor cold."* They believed and accepted Jesus, but they weren't going to get all radical about it. They had life figured out. Jesus and Christianity were just a bonus, icing on the cake. It was as if they were saying: "Don't get all weird about it; just be a Christian and move on!"

The problem with that kind of thinking is that it literally sickens the heart of God. Jesus says to the apostle John in Revelation that he felt like he would vomit when he considers the lukewarm nature of the church in Laodicea. I have this exact concern for the church in the United States. We, like them, view ourselves as wealthy and accomplished. We have reached a level of comfort and status that we deem to be impressive and worthwhile. We view Jesus, Christianity, and the church as a bonus, an obligation, or, worst of all, a good luck charm. We hope to appease Christ enough so that when this life is over, we can go to heaven. We just don't want to apply Christ enough to our lives to actually change our way of living. We have become lukewarm, and I fear that we make God sick to his stomach!

Instead of being lukewarm, the apostle Paul is

"contending" with us so that we might be ...

"Encouraged in heart"

"The heart, in Biblical language, is not the seat of feeling only, but stands for the whole inner man, as the 'vital centre' of his personality" (Spence and Exell 1950, 82). The encouragement of heart that the apostle is contending for is a fulfillment of the vital center of personality within each believer. Not just that he might have hope and joy in his feelings, but that the Christian might be changed, moved, directed, and empowered from the very core of personality.

"United in love"

The apostle contends for Christians to be drawn together by the power of their faith in Christ. All too often, we are divided by our own definitions or opinions of the person of Jesus. Instead, the apostle Paul desires that we would be drawn toward one another in love. Honestly, we can divide humans in to all kinds of categories. Categories like gender, race, skin color, political affiliation, nationality, creed, age, and the list could be endless. If we could ever find freedom from our man-made divisions and see the world as God sees it, we would be able to see people through the lens of love. Jesus died for all people. Therefore, all divisions are no longer valid. Are you a follower of Jesus or not? This is a simple question. This question is completely unconcerned with any of the divisions we fight and worry over.

"The full riches of complete understanding, in order that they may know the mystery of God, namely, Christ, in whom are hidden all the treasures of wisdom and knowledge."

The apostle contends with the Colossians so that they might find a complete and mature faith in Christ. Some seem to think that belief in Jesus is elementary or only for the simple minded. However, the opposite is true. The longer that one considers the teachings of Christ, the sacrifice of Christ, and the person of Jesus who is the Christ, the deeper one's appreciation becomes for the person of Christ. Jesus is the pivotal point of all human existence. The teachings of Jesus have impacted everyone. The apostle Paul consistently contends for our understanding of Christ. In Jesus, the mysteries of life and death are laid bare and finally unraveled. It all can make sense when Jesus is at the center of it.

We must come to grips with this Jesus who is the mystery of God and the illumination of understanding truth. When we do, we can finally find within ourselves a union of the *"love"* that unites us in Christ and the *"wisdom and knowledge"* that enlightens us in Christ.

Day 2

"I tell you this so that no one may deceive you by fine-sounding arguments. For though I am absent from you in body, I am present with you in spirit and delight to see how disciplined you are and how firm your faith in Christ is. So then, just as you received Christ Jesus as Lord, continue to live your lives in him, rooted and built up in him, strengthened in the faith as you were taught, and overflowing with thankfulness." (Colossians 2:4-7)

"Fine-sounding arguments"

Again, the apostle here warns against being deceived by smooth talking people who are either lying to us or are confused. Just like the apostle Paul dealt with Gnosticism and other false teachings in his day, we face variations and corruptions of Christian and biblical doctrine and understanding today. There is no shortage of people with opinions about the Bible. (There is a real shortage of people with opinions about the Bible who have actually read the Bible!) At every turn, on millions of web pages, in chat rooms, bars, restaurants, and town halls, people have opinions about Jesus. Some of them formulate their opinions into what amounts to a new form of theology. This proliferation of ideas is complicated by our tendency to follow anyone who can make a convincing argument.

The apostle warns us against such things. Don't be deceived by *"fine-sounding arguments."* Test the truths people speak into your life against the truth of God's Word. Remember, we have been given God's Word in the Bible. Through the Bible and guidance of the Holy Spirit, we can find the wisdom and knowledge we need to defend ourselves against smooth talking liars.

"Disciplined"

The Greek word for "discipline" is the word "taxis." Strong defines it as "due or right order; orderly condition" (Strong 2010, 247). In other words, the apostle Paul has heard reports that these folks are falling in line with solid teaching, keeping themselves free of false doctrine, and arranging their lives and congregations in such a way as to defend the truth. In his absence from them, he is delighted to hear that they are still holding strong. We should take note here. Our faith should not be treated as a trinket or good luck charm. It should be practiced in "due or right order" and in an "orderly condition." We should be building consistent practices that keep our faith fresh and strong. Prayer, Bible reading, small groups, worship services, retreats, all of these help to build our faith and keep us strong.

"Rooted and built up"

The Christian should be building in two directions at all times. We should be striving to reach for the sky with our Christian walk and our church. We must also be striving to reach even deeper in our own personal faith and relationship with Christ. Here in Maryland, my wife and I live in a house that is largely in the woods. Every so often, I must bring in a tree specialist and consider the trees that may threaten our home during a storm. The tree specialist considers two things. First, he assesses if any of the trees close to my house are dead or dying; those get taken down. The other assessment is of healthy trees. A species of tree that does not have a deep and strong root system is cut down, even though it may be healthy. Its health does not pose a threat to my home, but its lack of deep roots does pose a threat. That type of tree is built up but not rooted and is therefore dangerous. Christians are like that. Some are built up tall and impressive, but they lack deep roots. Without deep roots, storms come and topple them over. In the aftermath of their falling, homes are broken, relationships are crushed, and churches are destroyed. We absolutely must be growing in two directions at all times. We must be reaching for the greatest height that the Holy Spirit would lead us, all the while reaching the greatest depth of rootedness in the life-changing power of God's Word and presence.

"Strengthened in the faith"

Strengthening one another in faith is what we do every week in church. Twice a month, I sit with a group of pastors. We all work in the same network of churches attempting to reach our region with the gospel. We come together to contemplate and write our sermons. I often will remind them of a simple truth the Holy Spirit taught me when I first started in ministry. I was intimidated at the thought of preaching the Word of God to people who had been in church longer than I had been alive. As I was wrestling with this one afternoon in the church I pastored, I sensed the Holy Spirit give me a truth: "Michael, it is not your job to say anything new. That would be heresy. It is your job to remind them of what they should already know." Brilliant!

That is what we do when we all come together in church for worship and preaching. We are not really here to learn anything new, at least not those who have been in church a long time. We are here to be reminded of what we already know. Sometimes we have complete faith in God's Word, but we forget to remember and practice some part of it. When we come together in worship, we are reminded of those parts that we have somehow neglected and are challenged to strengthen our faith in that area once again.

"Overflowing with thankfulness"

Here is the outcome of the matter. I find it odd when Christians are negative about their life, especially western Christians. In our developed world, we don't face imprisonment or danger just because we gather and worship together. We don't face hunger and deprivation like so many in our world. We don't lack opportunity to meet with God's people to worship Him and learn from His Word. So why are we not thankful? We seem to forget that our sins have been forgiven and the price of our sin has been paid. We are free from guilt, and we are filled with the Spirit of God. We have so much for which to be thankful. It is amazing that we would find time to begrudge something we think we should have, and yet we do. The outflow of the mature Christian life is gratefulness.

Thank God we have been forgiven.

Thank God we have provisions.

Thank God we can go to church freely.

Thank God we have an eternal hope of heaven.

Thank God!

Day 3

"See to it that no one takes you captive through hollow and deceptive philosophy, which depends on human tradition and the elemental spiritual forces of this world rather than on Christ." (Colossians 2:8)

When my wife and I were in our first two years of college, we were both studying music education at a state university. On the weekends, we would often travel with a group of friends and sing at various churches around our area. One afternoon while at the University, the topic of our little singing group ministry came up. One of our fellow students looked at me with obvious disgust in his expression and asked, "Why would you use music to promote fairy tales?" I was taken aback. I had never really been challenged like that before. I kindly moved on in the conversation and did not address what I saw as a rude offense to my belief system.

I learned something that day.

The world prefers *"hollow and deceptive philosophy"* to deep and meaningful theology.

That day, my fellow student was simply openly expressing what many of my other fellow students believed quietly. They felt that we were silly to believe in the God of the Bible. They would have felt it was silly to believe in any god. They preferred philosophies that gave them the freedom to act out in ways the Bible did not. They felt this freedom was wiser than my fairy tale. However, that philosophy actually turns out to be *"hollow and deceptive."*

Many have followed the philosophies of this world only to find themselves anything but free. The world's thinking opens a person up to addictions, diseases, broken relationships, confusion, and a broken heart. Those are the natural endings to many of the freedoms the world touts, yet they keep chasing them. One marriage doesn't work, so they dispose of that commitment only to enter into another one. They never deal with the brokenness that ended the first marriage. One weekend of partying ends with a wicked headache and a list of regrets only to be followed by another. One job doesn't bring fulfillment, so another is pursued only to find no fulfillment in that one either. The philosophies of this world are hollow and empty.

You don't have to live that way.

None of these bring hope. McGee describes the meaningless human philosophy well when he says, "False philosophy is like a blind man looking in a dark room for a black cat that isn't there—there is no hope for its search for truth" (McGee 1983, 350).

When philosophers look for meaning and truth outside of the reality of God, they are truly searching in the dark for a black cat that isn't there. Without a Creator, a Designer, a God, there simply cannot be meaning. If we are truly the result of millions of accidental or incidental collisions of elements and atoms, then meaning is not to be found. If we just happened by chance, then we did not happen on purpose. If we did not happen on purpose, then we cannot possibly have real purpose and meaning in life. This is the failure of worldly philosophy. It is looking for meaning while seeing the world as a series of meaningless occurrences and accidental anomalies. It just doesn't work.

Meaning and purpose are found in Christ!

Think back to chapter one of this book. As we unpacked the reality of who Jesus is, we found hope in Him as our Creator. We clearly came to understand that the God who made us loves us, and He is in control from the beginning to the very end. This means that we have purpose. God the Father, God the Son, and God the Holy Spirit had a plan from before the beginning of time. That plan included you and me. That plan gives my life meaning and purpose. If I was made for a purpose, then I can find my purpose. This is the profound difference between the philosophies of the world and the theology of the Bible.

The world seeks meaning from meaninglessness.

Reason from randomness.

Fulfillment from emptiness.

Christian theology is entirely different.

It finds meaning in a Maker.

It finds reason in a Designer.

It finds fulfillment from the Father.

So take care as you walk in this world. Do not be deceived by people who sound smart but are selling hollow and empty thoughts and philosophies. They may hold teaching positions and degrees. They may be revered by the world as brilliant. They may speak in beautiful and compelling words. In the end, they are peddling emptiness. They will lead you to meaninglessness. Their hope is entirely hollow.

Meaning and purpose are found in Christ!

Day 4

"For in Christ all the fullness of the Deity lives in bodily form, and in Christ you have been brought to fullness. He is the head over every power and authority." (Colossians 2:9-10)

Have you ever felt less than adequate to face a given moment or situation in your life? If you have, then that makes you normal! We all face moments like this. This verse gives us a great deal of comfort in those overwhelming moments. It tells us two major truths. Jesus is God, and Jesus gives us power and authority.

Jesus is God

The Greek word used in this verse as *"fullness"* is pleroma. This word carries a number of shades of a single meaning — full; complete; abundance (Strong 2010, 204). The apostle is declaring without any doubt that Jesus is completely God. There have been people throughout the existence of the church who claim that Jesus is less than God. Here in Colossians, the apostle is declaring them wrong. He wants us to know that Jesus is completely, fully, and abundantly God. He is God the Son. While it is difficult or even impossible for us to fully grasp the concept of the Trinity, it is no less true. God the Father, God the Son, and God the Holy Spirit. Jesus (God the Son) is unique in all of history. He is 100%

God AND 100% human. That reality is of absolute importance to us as Christians. As a result of Jesus being 100% human, He can understand everything we are going through. He had the right to pay the price for the sins of mankind, because He became a part of mankind. His humanness is important to our ability to know Him and the Father. As a result of Jesus being 100% God, He holds the *"power and authority"* over anything and everything we may face in our lives. Jesus understands us and has the power to do something to help us!

Jesus is God!

Jesus Gives us Power and Authority

It is not enough to simply know that Jesus has power and authority over all things. It is imperative we understand that Jesus gives power and authority to us. Our verse today says, "in Christ you have been brought to fullness." His fullness dwells in me, even though I am unworthy to have such fullness. There is a word inside of theological circles that I would like to introduce here. The word is "imputed," which means to "put on." In theology, the term is mainly used to describe the righteousness of humans in the sight of God. The concept is simple. Since no human is actually worthy of the sacrifice and grace of Jesus, worthiness is "imputed" upon them. It is credited to (put on) them even though they don't actually deserve it. This imputed righteousness is what gives broken and sinful humans hope that they can be redeemed and holy followers of Christ.

Consider the same concept applied here. I do not have nor do I deserve to have the power to accomplish all God has called me to do for His glory. I can't think well enough, work hard enough, be talented enough, or learn nearly enough to accomplish the work the Holy Spirit desires to do in and through me. But Jesus chooses to make all of that different. I may still not be enough, but Jesus is more than enough. According to this verse from the apostle Paul, I *"have been brought to fullness. He is the head over every power and authority."* Spoken another way: "The fullness of Christ has been put on me even though I don't deserve it."

That's great news for everyone!

Let's go back to the question we started with today: Have you ever felt less than adequate to face a given moment or situation in your life?

It is impossible for me to describe every moment I looked around and realized just how inadequate I was for the work given to me by God. It happens almost every day. As I stand before a church filled with people or staff who are looking for occupational fulfillment and security, I am reminded I am not enough. As I looked into the faces of my children the day they were born, I knew I was not enough. As I look into their adult faces now and realize they need a role model who they can always look up to, I realize I am not enough. Over and over again, I realize I am not enough. However, over time, I have watched as the Holy Spirit (who always points to Jesus) gives me power when I need it. In other words, when I am not enough, Jesus is more than enough!

Let me shift your thinking a little here. Instead of being afraid of moments when you are not enough, consider this: When you find yourself on the edge of a situation where you know you are way over your head and completely inadequate, don't react with fear. React with excitement! At the end of **your** ability is the realm of **His** capacity! Since I am beyond my capacity, I am entering the realm of the miraculous.

Stop asking, "What can I do?" Instead, ask, "What can God do?"

Stop worrying that you are not enough. Simply settle into the fact that you are actually not enough. Then lean on the all-sufficient arms of Jesus and the ever-present power of the Holy Spirit and remember: *"For in Christ all the fullness of the Deity lives in bodily form, and in Christ you have been brought to fullness. He is the head over every power and authority.* "

So now, are you afraid?

Day 5

"In him you were also circumcised with a circumcision not performed by human hands. Your whole self ruled by the flesh was put off when you were circumcised by Christ, having been buried with him in baptism, in which you were also raised with him through your faith in the working of God, who raised him from the dead." (Colossians 2:11-12)

Ok, let's start with an awkward conversation ... circumcision.

Circumcision is the removal of the foreskin from the penis of a male. It is most commonly performed very quickly after birth and is practiced largely for religious reasons. While there are scholars and health experts on both sides of the debate over the benefits of circumcision, there seems to be some evidence of its health benefits.

A debate about the benefits or dangers of circumcision is not our point here.

In Genesis, God speaks to Abraham and makes this covenant with him: *"This is my covenant with you and your descendants after you, the covenant you are to keep: Every male among you shall be circumcised. You are to undergo circumcision, and it will be the sign of the covenant between me and you"* (Genesis 17:10-11). Then in verse 23: *"On that very day Abraham took his son Ishmael and all those born in his household or bought with his money, every male in his household, and circumcised them, as God told him"* (Genesis 17:23). This ancient practice became the mark of a son of Israel. It spoke of a promise God had made to the children of Abraham. It was a promise that they would remain God's people. This mark, once made, was irreversible. Everyone knew you were a child of Abraham, or at least could know by one simple mark.

In the New Testament, after the ministry, death, and resurrection of Christ and after the day of Pentecost, a debate arose within this brand new church. It was a debate about whether circumcision was to be practiced within the body of Christ, the Church. In Acts 15, the leaders of this infant church gathered in Jerusalem to decide what was required of converts to Christianity. Some were demanding that all males who converted should be circumcised. As you can imagine, this would have been a very real deterrent to men choosing to follow Christ! So the elders decided that not all of the Old Testament Law was necessary for those who were saved by the blood of Christ. (Acts 15:22-29 contains the letter they sent throughout the church.)

So why does the apostle Paul bring it up here?

Simple. Those folks who want to demand

adherence to Old Testament Mosaic Law are showing up in Colossae. They are leading some of the followers of Christ astray. The apostle Paul takes the opportunity to redefine circumcision in the era of the redemptive work of Christ and the empowering work of the Holy Spirit.

"In him you were also circumcised with a circumcision not performed by human hands. Your whole self ruled by the flesh was put off when you were circumcised by Christ."

Circumcision was always a mark on the man who was committed to God. The apostle Paul contends that the mark placed on the follower of Christ will now be a spiritual mark rather than a physical mark. Instead of the priest cutting away the foreskin of a child, the Holy Spirit cuts away the sinful nature of an adult. That process of putting off your sinful nature is as equally dramatic, and often traumatic, as a physical circumcision! In fact, I am certain that some Christians would prefer the physical trauma, even as an adult, because it would be over quickly! The circumcision done by the hands of man is simply external. It does nothing to change the heart. It is an external, physical mark that the internal, spiritual self may or may not live up to. It is much like a tattoo that speaks of a former love interest or way of life that is no longer applicable, but it is nonetheless permanently marking the body. Circumcision did nothing but mark a man as a Jew, and we are now Christians.

The circumcision done by Christ is different. This reaches into the very heart and soul of a person, male or female, and changes them. The outward mark of this inward circumcision is the act of baptism. When we are baptized into the family of God, the imagery is actually stunning. As we descend beneath the water, we are *"buried with him in baptism."* As we rise up out of the same water, we are *"raised with him through your faith in the working of God."* Through the sacrifice of Christ and the power of the Holy Spirit, God offers us a deep spiritual mark that does not cut away flesh but rather cuts away sin. We are then marked by our actions, not by our bodies. We are set free … we are made new … we are changed … all by the blood of Christ and the power of the Holy Spirit!

Day 6

"When you were dead in your sins and in the uncircumcision of your flesh, God made you alive with Christ. He forgave us all our sins, having canceled the charge of our legal indebtedness, which stood against us and condemned us; he has taken it away, nailing it to the cross. And having disarmed the powers and authorities, he made a public spectacle of them, triumphing over them by the cross." (Colossians 2:13-15)

Let's take this one phrase at a time.

"When you were dead in your sins and in the uncircumcision of your flesh."

This is a vivid picture of what sin does to a human both physically and spiritually. Sin causes death. If we look back in Genesis and the Garden of Eden, we realize there was no death there in that perfect place. The Tree of Life was planted there and gave eternal life to all those who ate from it. God had but one rule, and Adam and Eve broke that rule. Sin entered the garden, and with it came death. To this day, sin is still causing death in and among us. Often as a pastor, people will come to me confused and sometimes angry. They will ask some variation of the same question: "If God is so good then why did this horrible thing happen?" In that moment, my job as a pastor is not to have a theological discussion about the devastating effect of sin on the human state. In that moment, I just sit and wonder with them while asking God to soothe the pain of so great a loss. But here, we should discuss it.

Death is caused by sin ... always.

It's not always the sin of the one who died or got sick. Sometimes the obvious sin of another person is the cause of death for an innocent person. For instance, a drunk driver, a murderer, a careless foreman, etc. Often death comes and there is no clear sinner to blame. Death has reign over us because of sin. Simply because of the sin of our ancient relatives, Adam and Eve, we are now subject to death, sickness, and sorrow. Our journey is clearly taking us back to Eden. This time, we will call it heaven and when we get there, we will understand what life really looks like. Life lived in the bright Light of Life and not in the dark shadow of death. It will be glorious!

"God made you alive with Christ. He forgave us all our sins, having canceled the charge of our legal indebtedness, which stood against us and condemned us; he has taken it away, nailing it to the cross."

The keys to that wonderful place are clearly held in the hands of Jesus (Revelation 1:18). Jesus made us (imputed upon us) alive! *"He forgave us all our sins"* ... all of them! He did not pick and choose and decide which certain sins were so vile that He would still leave those there. He forgave every sin past, present, and future. In fact, the apostle goes even further in his analogy on this matter. He shows us that Jesus *"canceled the charge of our legal indebtedness."* One commentator gives great imagery on this: "The ancients commonly used wax tablets in writing, and the flat end of the pointed stylus drawn over the writing smeared it out (expunged) and so cancelled it" (Spence and Exell 1950, p. 89). That is exactly what Jesus has done for us. He has "smeared it out" or "expunged" it. He has "cancelled" our sin. Our sin is gone. In Psalm 103:12, it declares this, *"as far as the east is from the west, so far has he removed our transgressions from us."* I heard one old preacher remind his audience that this east to west is in a straight line. Not a curved one, like rounding the planet earth. If the lines are curved, they will eventually meet again. Instead, God throws sin away in a straight line so that you never meet up with it again!

Jesus did all of this by His sacrifice for us on the cross.

Our freedom required His arrest.

Our comfort required His nails.

Our life required His death.

Jesus paid this price so that He could cast our sins away from us, *"as far as the east is from west,"* and make us new!

"And having disarmed the powers and authorities, he made a public spectacle of them, triumphing over them by the cross."

In Colossae, and much of Jewish thought of the day, there was a common practice of worshiping angelic beings (Spence and Exell 1950, 90). These angels were thought to have taken some part in creation. They were often worshiped, prayed to, or looked to for good fortune. Here, the apostle Paul makes it clear that these angelic forces were no match for the redemptive work of Christ. Christ *"disarmed"* them by virtue of being 100% God. He *"made a public spectacle of them"* by showing it was not their powers of good fortune that mankind needed, but rather the redemptive, sacrificial work of Christ. They falsely claimed to be able to give good fortune, while Jesus truly gave new life!

Day 7

"Therefore do not let anyone judge you by what you eat or drink, or with regard to a religious festival, a New Moon celebration or a Sabbath day. These are a shadow of the things that were to come; the reality, however, is found in Christ. Do not let anyone who delights in false humility and the worship of angels disqualify you. Such a person also goes into great detail about what they have seen; they are puffed up with idle notions by their unspiritual mind. They have lost connection with the head, from whom the whole body, supported and held together by its ligaments and sinews, grows as God causes it to grow. Since you died with Christ to the elemental spiritual forces of this world, why, as though you still belonged to the world, do you submit to its rules: 'Do not handle! Do not taste! Do not touch!'? These rules, which have to do with things that are all destined to perish with use, are based on merely human commands and teachings. Such regulations indeed have an appearance of wisdom, with their self-imposed worship, their false humility and their harsh treatment of the body, but they lack any value in restraining sensual indulgence." (Colossians 2:16-23)

There is an old saying that goes like this: "You cannot legislate morality." Politicians often use this phrase in order to bypass a moral law or regulation to which they disagree. On its face value, the statement is true. When my wife and I were teens, we attended a Wesleyan Youth Camp in North Carolina. The camp was held every year during the month of July. None of the dorm rooms were air conditioned nor was the cafeteria or the tabernacle (the meeting hall).

I did say we were in North Carolina in July, right?

Due to an old, long-standing legalism that had always been a part of the camp, no one was allowed to wear shorts in the tabernacle. So 300-500 sweaty teenagers sat and listened to a pastor preach with no air conditioning! I came to realize the real immoral position was the one that forced us all to wear jeans in that building. It is no wonder that so many of us fell asleep or snuck out to do anything but sit in that room! A couple of years later, Tina and I were on the leadership board for that camp and had the privilege of being part of the group who changed that rule. Morality demanded that we either allow those kids to wear more comfortable clothing or put air conditioning in that building. Since money was tight, we changed the dress code!

Christianity is always in danger of falling into silly debates. Sometimes people with good motives create rules that try to prevent others, especially young people, from straying too far from Christ. These rules are almost always well intentioned, but they get weird. The reason is simple. Real change in the actions of a person's hands requires real change in the attitude of a person's heart. Now, I am not opposed to rules. Rules are helpful boundaries that keep us safely on the right path. What I am opposed to is being overbearing or overpopulating with the rules we demand people to live under. Too many rules make us legalists or Pharisees. No rules give license to sin and leaves us empty, addicted, diseased, and broken. Rules are fine and often necessary, but they must be understood and applied in the limited areas where they can be helpful. Otherwise, they become ...

> *Rules, which have to do with things that are all destined to perish with use, are based on merely human commands and teachings. Such regulations indeed have an appearance of wisdom, with their self-imposed worship, their false humility and their harsh treatment of the body, but they lack any value in restraining sensual indulgence.* (Colossians 2:22-23)

The real question here is in verses 20-21: *"Since you died with Christ to the elemental spiritual forces of this world, why, as though you still belonged to the world, do you submit to its rules: 'Do not handle! Do not taste! Do not touch!'?"*

Why do we do this?

Why do we submit ourselves to overly restrictive, non-biblical rules that are *"based on merely human commands and teachings"*? I guess the simple answer is that we don't want to offend or be rejected by the folks who are in charge of our religious group. Every religious organization has these rules. They are designed to hold people in close to the Savior, yet what they often accomplish is to hold people down from their highest growth potential. Worse yet, they drive people away from the salvation that is so desperately needed in our culture.

We should take a lesson from the church fathers in Acts 15. They were facing a huge influx of non-Jewish people who came to believe in Christ, on the one hand, and a multitude of laws they had practiced their entire lives, on the other. The volume of Jewish law is daunting in the Old Testament alone. Add to that the centuries of additions put into place by teachers of the law and Pharisees, and you have what must have seemed like an impossible road map to God! So these early church leaders took volumes of laws created over centuries of time and boiled it down to this statement:

> *It seemed good to the Holy Spirit and to us not to burden you with anything beyond the following requirements: You are to abstain from food sacrificed to idols, from blood, from the meat of strangled animals and from sexual immorality. You will do well to avoid these things. Farewell.* (Acts 15:28-29)

That statement is the founding rule set for Christianity. It is shorter than any set of rules I know of in any organization. Perhaps in the absence of legislation, people begin to realize their need for the guidance of the Holy Spirit. Whatever the reason for that little list, what we need to learn is that our salvation is found in the death and resurrection of Jesus, and our guidance is found in the sincere following of the Holy Spirit and God's Word. Everything else is *"destined to perish with use, are based on merely human commands and teachings."* They *"have an appearance of wisdom ... but they lack any value in restraining sensual indulgence."*

WEEK 3

Day 1

"Since, then, you have been raised with Christ, set your hearts on things above, where Christ is, seated at the right hand of God. Set your minds on things above, not on earthly things. For you died, and your life is now hidden with Christ in God. When Christ, who is your life, appears, then you also will appear with him in glory." (Colossians 3:1-4)

One of the things I love about the Bible is the wonderful balance we find in its teaching. The apostle Paul has just written passionately about our freedom in Christ. *"Since you died with Christ to the elemental spiritual forces of this world, why, as though you still belonged to the world, do you submit to its rules"* (Colossians 2:20). Then just a few verses later in Colossians 3:1, we read about setting our *"hearts on things above, where Christ is, seated at the right hand of God."* Balance is key to our success in any endeavor. The process of becoming Christ-like is not different.

"Since, then, you have been raised with Christ."

It is absolutely true that we are free from worldly and earthly rules and regulations. Again, remember what the apostle told us in the last chapter, verses 21-22, when he said, *" 'Do not handle! Do not taste! Do not touch!'? These rules, which have to do with things that are all destined to perish with use, are based on merely human commands and teachings.*" He goes even further in verse 23 when he states, "*Such regulations indeed have an appearance of wisdom ... but they lack any value in restraining sensual indulgence.*" These rules and regulations often fail to help us, yet they almost always succeed in frustrating us. We are not delivered from our sin in order to be imprisoned in some arbitrary list of dos and don'ts.

We are free!

Once we are free from the list of things not to do ... what do we do?

"Set your hearts on things above ... Set your minds on things above."

Before we found salvation in Christ, we had our hearts set on the things of this world. We were chasing sensual desires. The rules and regulations the church and world were placing on us lacked *"value in restraining"* our pursuit of those sensual desires.

So what changes?

It's really so simple that it's amazing. Christ changes what we desire and thereby changes what we pursue. Instead of having our hearts set on worldly things (things that Jesus has forgiven us for and delivered us from), we set our hearts on things above.

Our hearts change first ... then our actions will follow.

When I was a teenage boy, I was very focused on chasing girls. I had my heart set on having a girl at my side at all times. This meant that I dated a lot of girls during my teenage years. Then one day, I realized that the girl I was dating was the one I wanted to keep. Her name was Tina, and I have been married to her for almost 30 years now.

Now let me teach you something very important about relationships.

When I decided that Tina was the girl for me and ultimately married her, I did not set my mind on not chasing other girls. I didn't wake up every morning and remind myself, "Mike, don't chase women today!" I didn't sit in restaurants or on beaches and constantly remind myself, "Mike, you can't have those women. Don't chase those women! Don't chase those women!" My life does not revolve around some strict adherence to a law that says, "Don't chase women." Now let's be clear; I don't chase women! In fact, I don't think about other women. I don't chase women because I am too busy loving my wife to even worry about other women. You see the shift in thinking? When I choose to love my wife and make her peace and happiness my central focus, I don't have time or desire to chase other women. I chase her!

I didn't change the fact that I chase ... I changed what I chase.

Before Tina, I chased women ... now I chase Tina.

Before Christ, I chased sensual desires ... now I chase Christ!

In reality, in my relationship with Tina, I *"died"* and my *"life is now hidden"* with Tina in my home.

In reality, in my relationship with Christ, I *"died"* and my *"life is now hidden with Christ in God."*

I changed what I was chasing, and that changed where I was going!

When Christ, who is your life, appears, then you also will appear with him in glory."

When we change what we are chasing, we change the direction of our lives.

If I am chasing worldly, sensual desires, I am running away from God. If I am chasing Christian, biblical, godly desires, I am running toward God. Changing my desires naturally changes my direction. Changing my direction naturally changes my destination!

Day 2

"Put to death, therefore, whatever belongs to your earthly nature: sexual immorality, impurity, lust, evil desires and greed, which is idolatry. Because of these, the wrath of God is coming. You used to walk in these ways, in the life you once lived. But now you must also rid yourselves of all such things as these: anger, rage, malice, slander, and filthy language from your lips." (Colossians 3:5-8)

In no way do I mean to imply that the Christian life does not require adherence to some basic rules of action and etiquette. Again, part of the beauty of the Scriptures is that it is a balanced lesson. Freedom is real ... but our pursuit of Christ and Christ-likeness must be just as real. I have often repeated the following phrase to my congregation:

Grace is huge! But holiness is required.

Grace does not negate the need for holiness. Jesus did not die on a cross in order to give us license to live in sin. Jesus died on the cross in order to give us forgiveness to live free from sin.

"Put to death, therefore, whatever belongs to your earthly nature."

We are clearly called to live godly lives. We are called to take that old nature and *"put to death"* everything in it. Modern thinking takes a different route. It looks to simply explain away the sinfulness of sin. People look for ways to manage or rationalize sinful behavior. They do not think there is a real cure for sinful behavior. And they are wrong! The cure for sinful behavior is to put it to death so that we might live in Christ!

Again, returning to my marriage. In a very real sense, I put to death my practice of chasing women other than my wife. I did not do this by practicing some super strength in order to manage my desire for other women. I did this by focusing my desire on the one woman I was going to spend my life with — Tina. In the same way, we don't put to death our sinful nature by practicing some super spiritual strength; we do it by focusing on the One who sets us free — Jesus. The list the apostle gives us, *"sexual immorality, impurity, lust, evil desires and greed, which is idolatry,"* is clearly a list of items that if left to do their work would replace Christ in our lives. We have a tendency to allow any or all of these items to reside at the center of our living and focus. When they become the center of our focus, they take the place of God in our lives. They actually become our god since they are the force that animates and empowers us on a daily basis. That is called idolatry. We must put them to death by changing our focus.

"Because of these, the wrath of God is coming."

Make no mistake here; Judgment Day will come. There will be a moment when God the Father sits on His throne and judges the living and the dead (Revelation 20:11-15). On that day, everything that is not covered by the blood of Christ will be revealed. We will face our Creator and our only defense will be the blood of Christ. It matters where you set your heart, because the direction your heart is focused in will determine the response you receive from God at the Judgment.

"You used to walk in these ways, in the life you once lived."

There is an obvious turning point in the life of every believer. It is often, but not always, marked by a moment of surrender at a church service, event, or in the presence of a believer who led us to make a decision for Christ. However someone came to that turning point, it is there. Now you can say that *"you used to walk in these ways, in the life you once lived."* Don't miss the assumption here. That verse necessarily means that you currently walk in another way in the life you now live. Something has changed, and that something is Jesus! Your focus on Him has completely changed your direction.

"But now you must also rid yourselves of all such things as these: anger, rage, malice, slander, and filthy language from your lips."

I suppose there are no comprehensive lists of things we should or should not do in our pursuit of Christ. There are some obvious things that must change. A follower of Christ, one who has decided to focus his or her heart on following Jesus, will avoid behaviors like the ones the apostle Paul lists here. This phrase is no less emphatic than the phrase used earlier. Earlier, the apostle asks to *"put to death"* a list of things, and here he asks to *"rid yourselves"* of the list of things. Understand again that this is not simply finding a method to manage these things. Through the forgiveness of Christ and the empowerment of the Holy Spirit, we are to actually get rid of these kinds of actions and reactions.

This kind of living is almost never instant. It almost always requires time. It takes time to shift your direction. It takes time to break old habits and establish new ones. It takes time to change a life. And it takes love. Back one more time to my marriage. Tina and I fought a lot those first few years, but we never gave up. These days, almost 30 years later, we fight very little. Why? We have really come to know one another. With that, we instinctively know what we should say or do as well as what we shouldn't in order to have a peaceful home and loving relationship. In the end, what we have with Jesus is not a religion. It's a relationship. We do not put to death certain things in our lives in order to practice a religion. We do not rid ourselves of certain things in order to display religious purity. We put to death and rid ourselves of these things in order to bring joy to the heart of the Savior we love.

Religion is tough, even impossible, because it seeks to change the heart by controlling the hands.

Relationship is better, even joyful, because it seeks to change the hands by focusing the heart!

Day 3

"Do not lie to each other, since you have taken off your old self with its practices and have put on the new self, which is being renewed in knowledge in the image of its Creator." (Colossians 3:9-10)

"Do not lie to each other."

Truthfulness is one of the most desirable traits one can find in another person. All too often, this habit of lying invades the church. We embellish the statistics, stash some money for a pet project, or fail to expose the weaker parts of the church. Sometimes it plays out in very personal terms but with the same results. We embellish our accomplishments, act as if we give more than we do, or fail to admit the weaknesses that plague us. Lying is simply deadly among the body of Christ, and we should simply not do it.

I have been amazed over the years at the prevalence and acceptance in our culture of the lying nature of our politicians. I remember in the heat of a scandal involving then President Bill Clinton, I was talking with a family member who was defending what I considered indefensible actions of the president. I said, "You would throw me out of my pulpit if I acted that way. Do you really expect more of me than you do of the President of the United States?" The answer was shocking to me. "Yes. I do. He is a politician and you are a pastor. I expect more out of you." On the one hand, that is intensely unfair. Decisions made by the president have mortal consequences, and we should therefore attempt to find people of absolute integrity to hold that office. (Wouldn't that be nice?) On the other hand, I sort of understand. He is a politician; I am a pastor. We start at different places, so we arrive at different moral destinations. I start from a heart that has been set free by the blood of Jesus and journey forward through the care and power of the Holy Spirit. I suppose (though I don't really know this to be true) that a politician starts with a big dream to be president and journeys forward with successes and failures through the power of his or her own personality and funding.

These are very different. So I guess it's fair that the expectations are very different. May I suggest that these higher expectations are not just for the pastor? Every Christian should tell the truth. Every believer should be trustworthy, faithful, and true. Since we have been cleansed by Christ and filled by the Spirit, we should be changed people!

How much change is necessary?

Complete change is necessary!

"Since you have taken off your old self with its practices."

This is why my family member reacted the way he did, and it is why the world around you will react unfairly toward you as well. As a pastor, I have experienced the grace of Christ and immersed myself in the Word of God. Hopefully, I have tapped into the power of the Holy Spirit. Therefore, I have taken off the old self. As a politician, there is no requirement of such change. So one should always be able to trust a true Christian to tell the truth. This is not because of an arbitrary law, but because of a life-changing transformation of self. The old self was committed to chasing sensual desires, personally living well no matter the effect to the community, and seeking my best above and beyond anyone else's needs.

That was who I used to be.

Now I am someone different!

"Put on the new self, which is being renewed in knowledge in the image of its Creator."

The image here is of one being reborn. It is an image that the apostle Paul uses often. Jesus even used this imagery when He said, *"Very truly I tell you, no one can see the kingdom of God unless they are born again"*

(John 3:3). So the message here is simple and profound. When you surrender your life to Christ, you are given a brand new start. Every day we walk with Him, we are being renewed in His image. Every minute of exposure to His Word and His presence, we are being renewed. As long as we are on this side of heaven, we never stop being renewed by the power and presence of God.

I have traveled to a number of mission fields during the course of my ministry. Often, I find myself on these trips going to places that lack basic running water or electricity. I might spend days or even a week or more in the same set of clothes. Since there is nowhere safe to wash, I may go without bathing as well. Eventually, I always find myself in a place where running hot water and electricity are available. When I arrive back at those places, I go into my room and shed those old, dirty clothes. They stink and are stained with the residue of whatever it is we have been working on. I take the old off. I then get into the warm embrace of a clean shower. You would be amazed at how wonderful a shower in clean, warm water is after you have not had access to it for a week or so! Once I have cleaned my body, I put on new, clean clothes. I walk in feeling filthy and less than human. I walk out a new man — transformed and clean.

This is the testimony of the follower of Christ. I

was tired, dirty, stained, stinky, and felt less than human. Then I found the warm, cleansing power of the Savior of the world, bathed in the all-encompassing shower of the Holy Spirit, and now I am new.

A new creation ... a new self ... in the image of my Creator!

Day 4

"Here there is no Gentile or Jew, circumcised or uncircumcised, barbarian, Scythian, slave or free, but Christ is all, and is in all." (Colossians 3:11)

The apostle Paul makes a statement that is shocking and, likely, offensive to most of his readers. He suggests that the blood of Jesus negates all human divisions placed between people. This is profound! This is unheard of! This is shocking! Notice that there are eight distinctions. We can place these eight in to four different groups as suggested by the writers of the Pulpit Commentary: "The four pairs of opposed terms represent distinctions (1) of race [Gentile or Jew], (2) of religious privilege [circumcised or uncircumcised], (3) of culture [barbarian, Scythian], (4) of social rank [slave or free]" (Spence and Exell 1950, 151). When we see the four groups, we suddenly can overlay this teaching from the first century directly on our own social experience today.

There is no Gentile or Jew — Racial Division

While it is true that we have lingering divisiveness based on racial distinctions in our culture today, it seems to me that it hardly compares with the literal hatred that existed in the New Testament era.

The Jews were under the control of the Romans as was most of the known world at the time. They were not happy about it. These Romans had come in and militarily conquered the land and imposed much of their law and taxes on the people who wanted nothing to do with them. So the Jews tended to hate the Romans. The Romans, on the other hand, were the dominant force in the world at the time. They would overrun and destroy any and all military challengers seemingly with ease. So the Romans tended to look down on the Jews. The Jews had been named God's people all the way back in Genesis, and so they viewed themselves as special in the eyes of God. So the Jews tended to look down on the Gentiles (non-Jewish people). These Gentiles were everyone who happened to be non-Jewish, so they tended to be offended once they realized the Jews saw themselves as somehow special. The Jews hated the Samaritans — people who were part Jewish but not fully Jewish. And the list of divisions could go on and on. But Jesus changes all of that! Jesus paid the price for all races.

There is no Circumcised or Uncircumcised — Religious Privilege

This division is front and center in our current world. When any single religious group decides that everyone outside of that particular religion is somehow less worthy of life, land, freedom, or survival, then we have a huge problem. We fight these battles every day on a much smaller scale, even within Christianity. The Baptists struggle to get along with the Pentecostals. The Pentecostals don't think the Lutherans are on track. The Lutherans can't figure out the non-denominationalists. The non-denominationalists rebel against the denominations. Let's not even get started on the Catholics!

It's all a bit silly.

It would be funny if it weren't so dangerous. In Christ, these divisions are taken down. Jesus died for the sins of all humans, and that includes humans who believe in other doctrines, other denominations, and even other gods. Anyone who will set aside their own preferences and come to Christ find level ground at the foot of His cross.

There is no barbarian or Scythian — Culture

As the apostle writes these words, these two titles would refer to two particularly uncivilized groups of people. The barbarians were non-Greeks and therefore viewed as less educated and civilized as the dominant Greco-Roman population. The Scythians were even worse. McGee describes them this way: They "were probably the most barbaric the world has known. You talk about pagan, heathen, brutal, and mean! They would take their enemies and scalp them; then they would use the skull as a cup and drink the blood of their victims out of the skull!" (McGee 1983, 358). So the apostle Paul wants us to understand that with His sacrifice on the cross, Jesus bridges even cultural barriers.

There is no Slave or Free — Social Rank

Finally, there is no social ranking of persons. While we don't practice any formal division of social classes in our culture today, there is an assumed division. While we do not enforce this with laws, we do enforce it with price tags. I once read this phrase in a travel magazine while on a plane: "Privacy is the ultimate luxury." The article then went on to inform the reader that if one was willing to put in enough money, you could have all the service and privacy in the world, but it did not come cheap! Jesus isn't like that. There is no first class section on the salvation plane. In Christ, the civilized are on level ground with the uncivilized. The same goes for the educated and uneducated, sophisticated and uncouth, and rich and poor. In Christ, all social classes are brought to the level ground at the foot of the cross.

One of my favorite things about pastoring New Life Church, where I have had the honor to serve since January of 1999, is the multicultural and multiracial makeup of our congregation. To be honest, we really didn't plan on that. We never sat down and said, "Our goal is to be multiracial and multiethnic." We just wanted to reach people. And so, as the population around us began to integrate, our congregation integrated as well. We didn't focus on reaching white, black, brown, Asian, Middle Eastern, Caribbean, Southern, or Northern people. We just focused on reaching people. When you just focus on the category of human, you get all kinds. Simply put, skin color is of no distinction. We are all washed clean through the red blood of our precious Savior!

Day 5

"Therefore, as God's chosen people, holy and dearly loved, clothe yourselves with compassion, kindness, humility, gentleness and patience. Bear with each other and forgive one another if any of you has a grievance against someone. Forgive as the Lord forgave you. And over all these virtues put on love, which binds them all together in perfect unity." (Colossians 3:12-14)

Here we are with the clothing thing again! This time, we are not being instructed as to what clothes to take off. Those dirty rags we were wearing when we met Christ are already gone! Now the apostle wants to make sure we know what we are to be wearing from here forward. What a contrast. We were called to discard things like sexual immorality, impurity, lust, evil desires, greed, anger, rage, malice, slander, filthy language, and lying. Now we are called to put on the clothes of compassion, kindness, humility, gentleness, patience, forgiveness, and love.

Consider something I think is a really amazing truth in Scripture. If we live out our lives practicing compassion, kindness, humility, gentleness, patience, forgiveness, and love, then we will, without trying, live out the verses that precede these. We will naturally view all humans with value and the level of dignity that Christ demands of us. Consider these terms.

Compassion

When you look up this word in a Greek dictionary, it is described by words like "pity" and "mercy" (Strong 2010, 177). You find it referencing a deep-seated heart of compassion that is compelled to help others and make the lives of those who are suffering easier. In other words, this is more than just feeling sorry for someone; this is a deep compassion that requires action.

Kindness

This word in Greek is described using words like "moral goodness" and "integrity" (Strong 2010, 273). This is a real and natural kindness that should be welling up from the heart of a believer.

Humility

I love the descriptive phrases for humility, especially this one: "A deep sense of one's moral littleness" (Strong 2010, 247). Wow. That sums it up. Much of the trouble we create for ourselves stems from a sense of our own importance. Christians should operate from a sense of security in Christ, and a sense of smallness in the overall work of Christ. Grateful for the small role we have been allowed to play while not being overly impressed with that same small role.

Gentleness

This one uses the descriptive phrase, "mildness of disposition" (Strong 2010, 209). The image I have is the way one would pick up a tiny kitten. While many people don't like cats, everyone loves a kitten. They are small, frail, and soft. Therefore, when you pick up a small kitten, you do so gently, softly, slowly, and kindly. What would the world around us be like if we handled people with that kind of gentleness?

Patience

This word gets a lot of descriptions: "Endurance, constancy, steadfastness, perseverance, forbearance, longsuffering, slowness in avenging wrongs" (Strong 2010, 155). We really do lack this one! All you have to do is drive a crowded highway and patience is gone! Folks show all sorts of ungodliness to fellow drivers on the highway with their "I Love Jesus" bumper sticker on the back of their vehicle. Patience would be a great add to every godly life.

Forgiveness

The Greek word for forgiveness is defined as, "To grant forgiveness or pardon" (Strong 2010, 270). Now this one can be really tough. When people have hurt us or done us wrong, it can be extremely difficult to pardon or grant them forgiveness. Strong also uses this phrase, "To do something pleasant or agreeable." That's the last thing we want to do for someone who has hurt us. Interestingly enough, the apostle Paul clearly says, *"Forgive as the Lord forgave you."* He used the exact same word for forgive! Jesus is not asking anything from us that He has not already granted to us.

Love

Here it is. We land on the Greek word "agape." It has been defined as unconditional love (Strong 2010, 2). Love that one gives even to those who don't deserve any love at all. This is the love that loves the unlovable. This is the love that God shows for us.

What would our world be like if we were clothed in these attributes? Literally wrapped up in compassion like it was some warm, soft scarf on a cold winter day. Covered over with a beautiful shirt of kindness and soft pliable pants of humility. Our hands covered with the gloves of gentleness for the soft handling of others. Our feet covered with shoes of patience that have no need to rush in. Our arms encased in forgiveness and always ready for the needed hug that says, "It doesn't matter what you've done; you are welcome here." All of this covered over with the amazingly soft and beautiful overcoat of love.

What an outfit. What a beautiful outfit that would be.

What a beautiful person that would be.

A follower of Christ.

Day 6

"Let the peace of Christ rule in your hearts, since as members of one body you were called to peace. And be thankful. Let the message of Christ dwell among you richly as you teach and admonish one another with all wisdom through psalms, hymns, and songs from the Spirit, singing to God with gratitude in your hearts." (Colossians 3:15-16)

This is a perfect picture of what a church family should look like!

A Body Ruled by Christ

The Church is the body of Christ in this world. We are the hands and feet of Christ to a world that does not yet know Him (1 Corinthians 12). The leading thoughts and passions of the body of Christ must be about the Christ who is our head! All too often, we get caught up in other things that distract us from the Christ we are here to serve. Some churches get caught up in politics and others in social works. Some get caught in the production of a big show and others in their own tradition and liturgy. Churches can get caught up in family disputes and legal battles, arguments over hymnals and carpet color, and debates over liberalism, conservatism, creationism, and any other "ism" you can think up! But it's not about any of that! The church should ... no ... the church must be about Christ! We are a body ruled by Christ, and we should be a people pointing the world to Christ.

A Body of Peace

Peace should be the hallmark of the church as it points people to Christ. I have been around churches my entire life. I have seen church feuds and congregational fights that would rival a bad soap opera. It just shouldn't be like that. The people of God should not be fighting with each other, especially not in the courthouses of the world (1 Corinthians 6:1-8). Somehow the very people who are preaching the sacrificial love and forgiveness of the Savior of the World have found it impossible to actually sacrifice and show forgiveness. I don't mean to be insensitive, but moments like that make me question the very salvation of those involved.

A Body of Thankfulness

We have so much for which to be grateful. While the world around us flounders in its own sin and lost-ness, we have hope. We have hope for a better life here and hope for eternal life on the other side of death. We carry a hope that the world cannot even understand. Some live in the religious insecurity of a pantheon of gods and demigods who fight amongst each other and do not care for the humans who worship them. Some live in the religious hatred of a god who calls for the destruction of everyone and everything that is different. Some live in the religious theology of atheism where their very existence is a cosmic mistake and purpose and meaning are ridiculous fantasies. We follow a God who created all things with purpose and meaning (Genesis 1), and implores us to love our enemies and do good to those who harm us (Matthew 5:44). We follow a God who is the one true, loving, and merciful God of Heaven (Deuteronomy 6:4).

We should be thankful for all God is and all God has done on our behalf!

A Body of Learning

There is so much to know about God and His Word. We could never *"teach and admonish one another"* enough to actually gain true understanding of even the train of his garment (Exodus 33:12-23). The pursuit of the knowledge of God consumes some as they become theologians and scholars, but it should invigorate all. We all need to know as much as possible about this Creator who loves us so much that He gave His own life for us.

A Body of Praise

Worship is such an abused word, yet it can be so simple. We have boiled it down to little more than the music that happens before the preacher speaks. But worship is so much more! Our worship can be all-encompassing. Music is a powerful tool for worship. We sing at the top of our lungs because we hope that only a single note might reach the ear of God and bring Him joy. But there is more. We dance like a child in the presence of our Father to bring a smile to the face of an adored parent. We serve in hopes that our small investment of time and energy could somehow advance the work of the God we love. We give just a portion so that we can give thanks to the God who has given us everything we will ever have or enjoy. We stand in the awesome moment when the sun sinks below the horizon weeping at the beauty beyond measure and the artistry that somehow was born in the mind of God. We laugh and love as we gather together as families and enjoy the moments that make our lives worthwhile.

All of this is worship.

All of life is worship.

God is worthy of it all!

Day 7

"And whatever you do, whether in word or deed, do it all in the name of the Lord Jesus, giving thanks to God the Father through him." (Colossians 3:17)

When I was 16 years old, I got my first job. I had interviewed with the manager at the local Pizza Hut, and the interview seemed to have gone well. However, I didn't get the job. A few days later, on a Saturday evening, the phone rang at our house. It was the manager at the Pizza Hut. Apparently, the dishwasher they had hired chose not to show up for work that night. So there was now a new opening, and this guy wanted to know if I could fill that opening. It was snowing outside that night, and so I looked at my dad to see if he would let me brave the snow and go get my first job. He said yes, and so did I. About 45 minutes later, I arrived at the Pizza Hut. The manager took me to the back of the restaurant and there stood my task. The place had been very crowded that night and no one had time to do the dishes. So I stepped up to multiple piles of pan pizza pans taller than me along with mounds of dishes, silverware, glasses, and serving dishes. I had honestly never seen so many dirty dishes in one place in my entire life. So I got to work. I wasn't angry or disillusioned. This job couldn't possibly have been beneath me. This guy was going to pay me to wash those dishes. I had been washing dishes at home my whole life, and my mother never paid me! It was an honor to wash those dishes.

No, really, it was an honor.

I knew how hard it was to find a job in those days. I had watched my dad struggle to find work, and I watched as he and my mom wrestled with balancing a budget off of a single income. I also knew something else. I knew I was a representative of Christ in that place. I don't want to overplay my spirituality here. I was still a stupid teenage boy. However, I had been raised to realize that no matter what job you were doing, you did it to the best of your ability, if for no other reason than to give praise to the name of Christ. The people there may have known I was a believer, or they would soon know. I didn't want to have to explain a poor work ethic in order to offer the hope of Christ!

So I worked, and I worked hard.

I kept that job for almost three years. By the time I quit to go to college, I was the assistant manager of that place. They would leave me, an 18-year-old kid, in charge of the restaurant and employees. They would leave me to balance the cash register, prepare the deposit slips, count the money, and make the deposit. Thousands of dollars each night, and they trusted me with it. That was exactly the kind of impression I wanted to make. I cannot say that I always showed the best witness while working there, but I can say that I tried and worked hard.

I think somehow in today's church world, we have missed this lesson. The apostle says it clearly, *"Whatever you do, whether in word or deed, do it all in the name of the Lord Jesus."* The world would be a different place if every Christian followed that simple command, especially Christians in the workforce. Every employer out there should be looking to hire a Christian. They should expect more from us, and they should get what they expect. They should think of quality, hard work, honesty, and reliability when they think of church folks. They should see in us what we see in Christ. Jesus has never failed us. He has never lied to us. He has never called in sick just to go to a concert or a party at the lake. Jesus is always faithful. Jesus didn't give us His least while He walked among us. He gave us His best.

We have just talked about worship and gratitude. A good work ethic is a form of worship. When we do quality work and people know we are followers of Christ, we worship the name of Christ by working like He worked. When they trust us, we bring glory to the name of Christ by being like Him. When they sleep peacefully knowing that we have their business covered, we bring glory to the name of Christ who has our future covered by His grace and mercy. Gratitude is what we should show when someone is willing to make us part of their dream, their world, their investment, their business. I must admit that I know nothing of working for a government agency or massive corporation. I have always worked for small businesses. When a small business owner hires you, he or she entrusts a portion of their life dream in your hands. You should be grateful for that. You should show your gratitude for that. I remember my first paycheck. It was awesome! I was amazed how much I obviously liked the government upon seeing how much I had given them! I was also amazed at how quickly money could disappear, but I was still grateful. I went back the next week and washed some more dishes ... to the glory of God!

WEEK 4

Day 1

Most of this week will be spent in a discussion about family relationships. The family dynamic is the very core of all social structure. Any culture with strong family structure will be a successful and strong culture. Any culture with broken family structure will ultimately fail. Family, a strong, healthy family, is imperative. We see this truth play out in so many cities and countries. There is great progress in social growth and strength in places where family is celebrated, encouraged, and strengthened. In numerous studies cited by familyfacts. org, it was demonstrated that students from intact family environments outperformed their peers from single family or blended family environments in literally every measurable area. Given that there are so many broken or blended families in our culture, the single greatest contributor to these issues was the weakened nature of the family unit.

Now, let's be fair; there is no need to panic or disparage anyone who is in or part of the creation of a broken, single parent, or blended family. My wife and I both come from blended families. My parents divorced when I was around two years old. The idea that non-traditional family units are less than ideal is not my point here. My point is that whatever family you have at the moment is worth fighting for and worth maintaining!

In our current cultural setting, marriage and family is being treated as a second tier issue. Marriage is increasingly being viewed as something to be put off as long as possible or simply avoided altogether. One study by the Pew Research Center was cited in an article by cheatsheet.com as indicating that the rate of "never marrieds" in the country has more than doubled between 1960 and 2010. It also stated that an increasing percentage of those "never marrieds" are fully content with their singleness as a permanent life state. Now this should not be viewed as an odd or frightening statistic on its own. One could simply argue that we have matured as a culture to allow individuals to be fully content as self-contained individuals. However, there is one glaring problem. The same article makes it clear that those who are in a married relationship fare better in life in general.

So we have two conflicting yet true realities:

Marriage is good for people and society.

People and society are increasingly rejecting marriage.

Let me take the rest of this time to speak clearly about how God designed our lives to work. In Genesis 5:1-2, the Bible says this: *"When God created mankind, he made them in the likeness of God. He created them male and female and blessed them. And he named them 'Mankind' when they were created."* The very next verse begins to speak of Adam and Eve having children and raising those children. In Genesis 9:1, when Noah and his family finally get off the ark and back onto dry land, God commands them saying, *"Be fruitful and increase in number and fill the earth."* It has always been God's intent for men and women to marry, remain faithful to one another (I have not listed those verses here, but feel free to do a simple Bible search on your own. You will find God's opinion on the importance of faithfulness in marriage.), produce, and raise children. This is how the earth was designed to work from the beginning. It should not come as a surprise to us that society works best when people act in ways that are in keeping with how God designed us to thrive. Modern ideas that come against marriage are not modern at all. They have always been around. People like to rebel against structures, rules, and institutions. Marriage and family have all those. So from the beginning of time, some people have worked to diminish the importance of family. In perhaps the most recent and flagrant effort, Karl Marx openly advocated for the end of families within communist culture: "Abolition [*Aufhebung*] of the family! Even the most radical flare up at this infamous proposal of the Communists" (Marx and Engels 2016). I don't think it's really necessary for me to elaborate on the magnificent and devastating failure of communism in the twentieth century. This philosophy generated more death and slaughter of its own people than all multi-national wars combined throughout history! Today, communism is a completely failed form of government, even though it has been altered to resemble something more akin to totalitarian controlled capitalism. Every culture that has attempted to delete or undermine the central structure of the family has and will continue to fail.

So, family matters to God. Family matters to society. Family should matter to us!

In the next few verses, the apostle Paul speaks of family relationships and then of more general relationships. As he speaks, we should make it a point to take note of all he has to teach us and then work diligently to apply these lessons in our lives. Biblical truth applied properly will make our marriage better, our kids better, our homes better, our society better, and ultimately, our world better.

Day 2

"Wives, submit yourselves to your husbands, as is fitting in the Lord." (Colossians 3:18)

So much has been made of this phrase. This command is found here and in the letter to the Ephesians. The two letters were likely written during the same time frame. In Ephesians, the apostle Paul elaborates on the idea even farther: *"Wives, submit yourselves to your own husbands as you do to the Lord. For the husband is the head of the wife as Christ is the head of the church, his body, of which he is the Savior. Now as the church submits to Christ, so also wives should submit to their husbands in everything"* (Ephesians 5:22-24). Feminists have taken these verses to say that the Bible is forcing women into a subservient role in society, and some Christians agree with them. However, that isn't what the apostle Paul is doing at all.

All Scripture must be understood in the social and historical context in which it was written. When the apostle Paul was writing, women were not considered leaders in society. In fact, most societies of his day viewed women as little more than property to be owned and controlled by a given set of men. A woman was first owned and controlled by her father. Then she was owned by the husband chosen for her by the father. It was quite possible that a father would choose to give his daughter to a man who had multiple wives. The romanticized notions of Hollywood movies that show ancient women exercising great control over their surroundings would have been almost impossible for the vast majority of women. When the apostle writes these words, he is asking women to willingly choose to act in a given way toward their husbands. He does not follow the norms of his day, which would be to either ignore them or speak to them through the men that owned them. He speaks directly to them. The Gospel writers also established this pattern. In no logical plan would a first-century group of men admit that women played a major role in the formation and establishment of their religious beliefs. Jesus appears first to the women in all of the Gospels (Matthew 28:5-8, Mark 16:2-6, Luke 24:1-8, John 20:1). It is the women who take bold action and taught great lessons about anointing Jesus properly and with devotion (Matthew 26:6-13, Mark 14:3-9, Luke 7:36-50, John 12:1-8). Women consistently play an important role in this new Church that Jesus is establishing, and the apostle Paul is helping to shape it.

This brings us back to this command: *"Wives, submit yourselves to your husbands, as is fitting in the Lord."* I find two things extremely interesting here. First of all, I find it interesting that in both Colossians and Ephesians, the apostle gives a command to the wife and follows immediately with a command to the husband. There is an instant recognition that there are two parties with responsibility here. This would not have been normally true in the first century. The entire requirement of submission would have been to the wife. Here, we find a command for proper behavior given to the man as well. This is a departure from what would have been normal in this day. The apostle is clearly elevating the position of the wife by making the husband responsible as well! In our world, we miss that nuance. Today, all we hear is the word *"submit"* and alarms go off in our heads, and we immediately become defensive and angry. "How dare he suggest that my daughter submit to that man? How dare he insinuate that women should be submissive?" However, if we consider the historical context of the writing, we would understand that the apostle is doing just the opposite. He is elevating women, at least by the standards of his day.

Secondly, I find it interesting that modern psychology consistently teaches us that men need validation. Men especially need validation from the important women in their lives. Mothers, daughters, and wives carry an especially great amount of power over the men they raise, marry, and live among. To this day, and I am 50 years old as of this writing, I am convinced that if my mother angrily yelled at me, I would be emotionally crushed and just might melt into tears. Me! I intimidate people by accident, yet my mom could likely reduce me to tears. What's up with that? And she isn't the only one. My sister could do that. My daughter-in-law could likely do the same, though I've never even seen her angry. Then there's my wife! Wow. It would be virtually impossible for me to overstate the importance of my wife's approval in my life. If I were convinced that she disapproved of me or saw me as anything less than a good man, I'm not sure I would be able to effectively recover.

Now I know there are women and men who live in very different circumstances than mine. I know there are men who have done nothing to deserve respect, and women who have never learned to show respect. I realize there are some relationships that have developed to overcome these issues, and different people feel and react in different ways to different relationships. I get all that. But the core truth is no less true.

When wives honor their husbands, they make their husbands better men!

When wives honor their husbands, they make their husbands stronger men!

When wives honor their husbands, they, most often, make their husbands better husbands!

So, ladies, please don't read this verse or verses like it and think that God has it out for you, or that the apostle Paul was some kind of misogynistic beast. God loves you and wants the best for you. You are not being called to submission in these verses. You are being called to respect. In fact, as the apostle Paul is wrapping up his thoughts on this matter in Ephesians, he says, *"However, each one of you also must love his wife as he loves himself, and the wife must respect her husband"* (Ephesians 5:33).

Honestly, it's good advice.

Day 3

"Husbands, love your wives and do not be harsh with them." (Colossians 3:19)

Men, we are called to be good men.

I once heard a young man preaching on this passage and he said, "I find no call for submission for husbands, only wives." Well, I took note of his youth and assumed he would eventually understand the error of his ways. Likely his wife, who was present at the sermon and a strong, well-educated, and capable person herself, would set him straight once they got home! Men are called to a very deep and real partnership with their wives. Here the apostle gives the simple command to *"not be harsh"* with our wives. But he means so much more.

The letter to the Colossians was likely written during the same imprisonment when he wrote the letter to the church in Ephesus. So we can easily compare these two documents to get a fuller picture of what the apostle means when he calls men to *"not be harsh"* with their wives. In Ephesians, while dealing with the same subject in the same order and with many of the same words, the apostle elaborates:

"Husbands, love your wives, just as Christ loved the

church and gave himself up for her to make her holy,
cleansing her by the washing with water through the
word, and to present her to himself as a radiant church,
without stain or wrinkle or any other blemish, but holy
and blameless. In this same way, husbands ought to love
their wives as their own bodies. He who loves his wife
loves himself. After all, no one ever hated their own body,
but they feed and care for their body, just as Christ does
the church—for we are members of his body. 'For this
reason a man will leave his father and mother and be
united to his wife, and the two will become one flesh.' "
(Ephesians 5:25-31)

If you were paying attention when you read
that, you would realize that the apostle just laid down
some serious law! While wives are called to *"submit"* to
their husbands (read "respect"), husbands are called to
treat their wives just as Jesus treated the Church.

Guys … Jesus died for the Church!

He left the perfect place (heaven) to come to
a broken place (earth) to be less (human) to suffer
more (disrespect, misrepresentation, and beating) to
ultimately die (the cross) so that He could be buried
and rise again (Easter) so that we could be forgiven
and ultimately set free. Jesus did all of that to make us
better. Honestly, none of that made Him better. His
focus was on us. His focus was on our needs. This is the

example husbands are to follow in dealing with their wives.

Now, it is true that Jesus is God and is therefore perfect. It is also true that no mere man could ever actually completely accomplish this feat of selfless love. However, it does give us a standard that we should strive toward. This is what our relationship with our wife should look like. She submits to our need for respect, and we submit to her need to be cherished.

I like that word ... cherished.

I think that word would help a lot of men to shift their perspective in dealing with their wives. We should cherish our wives. I don't know what it is you cherish in life, but I do know something about how that cherished item gets treated. It is kept in a safe place. It is kept clean. It is kept well. It is guarded carefully. Those men who cherish cars will wash them, cover them, build expensive buildings to store them, lock them away, and NEVER drive them if there is a threat of rain! Every year at our church, we have held a classic car show. If there is even a chance of rain on that day, the event is canceled. No classic cars will show, because these people, mostly men, cherish their cars and will not risk driving them in the rain.

What if we treated our wives like that?

I don't mean we lock them in a garage and keep them out of the rain only to bring them out to show them off.

That's actually creepy!

I mean, what if we cherished them?

I find it interesting that modern psychology will tell us that most women need to know their husbands cherish them. Love them above all else, and find them to be beautiful and worthy of protection and honor. That is exactly what the apostle Paul commands of husbands! It is amazing when God's Word, seen by so many as irrelevant to our time, gets our current reality exactly right! And yet, it happens every time.

So, men, cherish your wife.

When husbands cherish their wives, they make their wives better women!

When husbands cherish their wives, they make their wives stronger women!

When husbands cherish their wives, they make their wives better wives!

Honestly, it's just good advice!

Day 4

"Children, obey your parents in everything, for this pleases the Lord." (Colossians 3:20)

Now this is a command that seems very far out of date!

I have often spoken to young people about the biblical role they are to play in their families. The sermon is honestly quite simple: "Honor and obey." Those two words sum up the commands of Scripture for children. Let's take some time to unpack the meaning of both words and perhaps apply them in a modern context.

Obey

The Greek word for obey is "hypakouo," and that word is defined in a number of ways. It can mean to listen; to harken; it can refer to one who hears a knock at the door, responds to the knock, and listens to the one knocking; to be obedient; or to submit (Strong 2010, 256). While all of these have a similar meaning, they do give some nuance on our understanding of obey. We can really put all of these in two different categories.

Listen

It is the work of children to learn. They are constantly in the process of learning about people and the world around them. The first place that learning happens is with parents. Children should listen to what their parents have to say. Parents as teachers are quite honestly underappreciated in our current culture. Parents have experienced much of what their children have yet to go through and therefore have a wealth of knowledge. This knowledge can and should be handed down. More importantly, parents have a love for their children that motivates them to teach rightly and consistently. While my children can learn life lessons from any number of experts, they will never learn from anyone more interested in their healthy development than their parents. That should be valued and leveraged far more often than it is in today's thinking. Children need to know and understand what their parents think and value. It will, most often, make them better.

Do

Once something is learned, it should be applied. Some lessons are negative. We learn what not to do. Some lessons are positive. We learn what to do. As the child grows and matures, he or she will be forced to make that determination. There are some things I learned from my parents that I have intentionally not repeated. Most things, I have intentionally applied, and it has made me a better person.

Honor

The word rendered as "honor" in Ephesians 6:2 is the Greek word "timao" and is defined as follows: "To estimate, fix value, to honor, to have in honor, to revere, to venerate" (Strong 2010, 250). We can apply these ideas in a given order. When we hear or observe something from our parents, we should automatically see it as having value simply because of where it comes from. However, there can be a process through which we can decide how to proceed with what we have learned from them. Consider this as a possibility:

Estimate the value of the lesson with honesty.

Not everything our parents say to us or model for us will be exactly the right thing for us to do. No human is perfect and therefore no parent is going to always be right. As children, we must estimate or consider the value of what we have been told, taught, or modeled from our parents and decide from there how to use that lesson. It is possible that our parents' lessons do not apply because of our new situation. My parents spent their lives in smaller churches usually with a single service and attendance of 50 to 250 per week. Today, I pastor a church with multiple locations and thousands in attendance. My parents' practice of church is not applicable to my situation. Their advice is not wrong; it's just not applicable. You may find yourself in a similar situation. Your parents live in a rural setting and you in an urban setting. Life lessons must be adjusted to fit your new reality. What doesn't change is the core truth of the lesson. In my case, the church is always about Jesus, biblically centered and based, and empowered by the Holy Spirit. While practices may be different, principles are not.

Honor the place from which it comes no matter what.

Even if your parents' advice turns out to not be usable, that should in no way alter the central command to honor your father and mother. Honestly, obeying them (or at least understanding and respecting what they want you to obey) is honoring them. By doing so, you honor their thoughts and their desire to help us develop as mature and productive humans.

So, kids (we are all at some stage of being a kid), obey your parents and honor them.

It really is good advice!

Day 5

"Fathers, do not embitter your children, or they will become discouraged." (Colossians 3:21)

Parenting is one of the toughest jobs on the planet, and it is one of the most difficult things we will ever attempt in our lifetime. It is very easy, especially as Christian parents, to overparent our kids and create strict rules that they become frustrated, or as the apostle says it, embittered with us. The balance here is so delicate and difficult. People have many different ideas on how to parent. I suppose you could fill your house with books on how to parent and each of them would have different advice. So what I would like to do here is just give you some short personal advice based on my experience as a father of three boys.

Start Strong and Then Lighten Up

In the beginning of a child's life, boundaries are paramount. "Don't touch that! Don't hit your brother! Don't put that in your mouth!" These are phrases you will use as a parent until you are tired of saying them! (You can understand why your kids are tired of hearing them!) When your kids are really young, you don't need to explain these commands at great length. These are boundaries of safety and caution kids need to learn in order to avoid actions that will bring them great pain or damage. We don't present them as questions or conversations; they are just commands, which is exactly what we need early on. Don't be afraid of these. Really young children don't yet possess the capacity for objective thought and reasoning. So give commands with authority and consistency.

When your children get older, they become more adept at objective and reasonable thought. As that ability arises within your children, engage it. Move away from short, terse commands and start having conversations. This doesn't mean the kid gets to make his or her own choices; it just means they get to take the thought journey with you. I have often looked at my kids when they were between the ages of 8 or 9 all the way up to 18 or 20 and said, "Look, you may disagree and we might find out I'm wrong in my thinking, but I am the parent and this is how it's going to work here and now. Once you are grown and gone, you can make your own choices." I've even been so transparent as to say, "When you leave my house, you will do whatever you want and I will have no say in that. But you haven't left my house yet. So between here and there, it's my job to make a good person out of you and this is the best way I know to do that."

The secret to this is doing it in the right order.

Some parents want to just play with their kids and be their friend until they become teens. Then, the stakes get really high and the bad choices get really dangerous. Then those friend-parents want to lay down the law for the first time. Their children have no idea what that is or how to react to it, and so they naturally rebel because "Dad just lost his mind!" You absolutely must start out strong and then let up. You cannot do it in reverse.

Have Fun

Now I am not suggesting that you should be so strict and strong with your young kids that you don't enjoy them. My boys are now grown and gone. While I am enjoying the empty nest with their mother, I do still miss them being around. I remember when our oldest left for college. I was fine. Mom cried but I was fine … until I got home. Once we were in the house, I had to walk past his bedroom door. Somehow in that moment, I realized he wasn't in there and I couldn't just go talk with him whenever I wanted. I lost it. It took me a good 45 minutes to get myself together. I was glad he was moving on and happy for who he was becoming, but something was missing in my house.

That's going to happen to you.

So while they are there, set rules, be firm, and have fun. Enjoy your time with them and make sure they enjoy their time with you.

Make Memories

Our American culture is desperately lacking in positive, life-affirming rites of passage, so I intentionally created some. My wife and I spoke when the boys were still quite young, and we decided I would take each boy on a father and son trip when they turned eight. On this trip, I would let them choose anything within reason they wanted to do. I would work to make what they wanted happen, and I would spend the entire trip just talking with that one kid.

It was awesome … all three times!

It was so great that I did it again at age 12. In fact, when they turned 12, we would go and buy them a gold necklace. Their mom would then put that necklace on them before we left for the 12-year old trip, and we would have "the talk" or at least what was left of the talk. (These days, most kids need to hear from their parents concerning sex and sexuality far before they hit puberty, much less before they turn 12!) I loved those trips, too. I loved them so much that I took each of them on an 18-year old trip as well. Today, we set two times per year when Tina and I will plan a vacation. We will see to it that there is room for everyone wherever we are going, and they will make plans to join us. These rites of passage have built within our family a strong sense of belonging and loyalty. We may not all see the world through the same lenses, but we all love each other and stand by each other at all times.

Return Honor with Honor

At a few points in our lives, one of the boys has had a public struggle. Each time, Tina and I would gather the other two around us and restate the obvious: "We may or may not agree with your brother right now, but we are going to stand together. Here and with our church and with our friends. Got it?" And they would always affirm that they understood. There is an old southern adage that goes something like this: "When you fight a southern boy, you can't just fight him. You gotta fight his whole family!" We kind of work that way. It's not a matter of fighting. It's a matter of honor. Today, our boys show great honor to their mother and me. I thank God for that. In return, we will show great honor to them. If tough conversations need to happen, they will, in private. To the world, you can't fight just one of us. If you come after one of us, you get us all!

Oh, and by the way, you want those kids to love and honor you. They choose your nursing home!

"Fathers, do not embitter your children." It's really good advice!

143

Day 6

"Slaves, obey your earthly masters in everything; and do it, not only when their eye is on you and to curry their favor, but with sincerity of heart and reverence for the Lord. Whatever you do, work at it with all your heart, as working for the Lord, not for human masters, since you know that you will receive an inheritance from the Lord as a reward. It is the Lord Christ you are serving. Anyone who does wrong will be repaid for their wrongs, and there is no favoritism. Masters, provide your slaves with what is right and fair, because you know that you also have a Master in heaven. (Colossians 3:22-25, 4:1)

Let's begin by thanking God that slavery is no longer an acceptable reality in our culture. There have been times in our country's past when it was. As Wesleyans, we are part of a great heritage. Our founders were on the forefront of abolishing the practice of slavery in the U.S. Our churches have been shot at and our pastors have been abused for their fight against slavery and bigotry. Thank God for His grace to all people and for giving us a new and better understanding of the inherent value of every human life. Just as a means of remembering, the apostle addresses such thinking in this very letter: *"Here there is no Gentile or Jew, circumcised or uncircumcised, barbarian, Scythian, slave or free, but Christ is all, and is in all"* (Colossians 3:11).

In our current cultural setting, the best application of this passage would be in the relationship between employers and employees. Specifically, let's look at employers of hourly wage earners, and even more precisely, companies that pay minimum wage. The minimum wage earner has very little power in his or her workplace. They are often the newest, least experienced, and least educated among the workforce. Their opinions and preferences are rarely taken very seriously. To be fair, it isn't wise for the owner of a corporation to put a great deal of emphasis on the thoughts and preferences of his lowest level workers. They are often there a limited number of hours and perform tasks of limited impact to the company. Focus should be on the workers who are there full-time and performing core tasks that keep the company healthy and productive. Now, what I just said is controversial in some circles. We have argued about workers' rights, company rights, the plight of the poor, and the rights of the wealthy for the entire existence of our nation. I'm not so certain that the answers here are not far simpler than all the laws make them out to be. Honestly, can we really pass more laws and believe that the new ones will be any better at making people value one another than the old ones? It's going to take something deeper and bigger than law. It's going to take God! With all of that being said, there are some things to be learned here.

Your Work is Christ Focused

To the worker, no matter where you are in the company, there is something here for you. *"Whatever you do, work at it with all your heart, as working for the Lord, not for human masters"* (Colossians 3:23). We often need to do the mental and emotional work of seeing each part of our lives from a spiritual vantage point. All to often, we relegate spiritual thought to our church time, devotional time, or even family time. We almost never allow spirituality to invade our work time or play time. The reason why is obvious. It changes everything! If I view my work time in the way the apostle Paul suggests, I see that some things are going to have to change. No more goofing off! No more fudging the time card! No more taking stuff home because, "I deserve it anyway." If I work as though I am working for Christ, I give it my all.

Honestly, it's not difficult to imagine working with all my heart for Christ! It is difficult to think about doing such a thing for my boss. Therefore, I need to change the way I think, and that will change the way I act, even at work.

Employers, your workers belong to Christ … just like you.

It's only right that employers should be held to the same scrutiny. It is incredibly difficult to work for employers who do not value their employees. When someone does not value your work, it is virtually impossible to value his or her need for your work to be of quality. Here is where the whole legal thing breaks down. You can't pass a law that requires someone to value another person. You just can't write a law that changes the way someone feels in his or her heart. Employers must value their employees from the heart. We just had an employee of our church move on to full-time work. She had served for five years as our receptionist. Every time I walked into the office building, she would smile and with a bright voice say to me, "Hey Pastor Mike!" She always seemed so glad to be there and so cheerful and encouraging. To some, her job may have seemed less important than, say, the bookkeeper, the counselor, the children's pastor, the youth pastor, or the senior pastor. But they would be wrong. Her bright smile and joyful attitude set the tone for everyone who entered our office. That was of great value to me and to everyone who worked there. She will be missed.

Some employers miss that. They don't understand the importance of the hourly worker, and they don't value the person that holds that position. This is a grave mistake on two levels. First of all, on a business level, it's a mistake because it is often the hourly worker that is the first face the public sees of your company. If that person feels devalued, they will show the world an image of your company that is not good. That can affect your company's ability to effectively operate. More importantly, this is a mistake on an eternal level. Every human is a child of God and deserves the respect of every other human. There are no small people. There are no throwaway people. There are only God's people. The higher you rise in any organization, whether it be of your own making or built by someone else, the more you must realize the value of all humans. God will hold you accountable one day for how you treated His creation, no matter how important you think they are. He thought they were important enough to die for on a cross.

Day 7

"Devote yourselves to prayer, being watchful and thankful. And pray for us, too, that God may open a door for our message, so that we may proclaim the mystery of Christ, for which I am in chains. Pray that I may proclaim it clearly, as I should. Be wise in the way you act toward outsiders; make the most of every opportunity. Let your conversation be always full of grace, seasoned with salt, so that you may know how to answer everyone." (Colossians 4:2-6)

As we come to the end of this epistle, it is appropriate that the apostle Paul turns our minds back to prayer. It is an absolute truth that nothing of value has ever been accomplished in the church without prayer. Prayer should be at the beginning, the end, in the middle, and all the way through everything we endeavor to do. Every lesson taught to us in this epistle should be put into practice and practiced with prayer. We should do everything with prayer. I am not just talking about the public and audible prayers we pray in our formal lives. Those are important. What I am talking about here and would like to wrap up with is an understanding of prayer as the very core and central theme of our existence. There is a phrase in the church world: "Bathed in prayer." I like that phrase. It gives the right mental image. It's not that I am going to pray for something before I start, though I should do that, or pray for something after it has ended, though I should do that as well. It's more like sinking my entire existence into a warm bath of prayer. Nothing escapes it. Just like a good bath, everything gets wet! The obvious parts and the covered parts get wet. The good, the bad, and the ugly get wet! That is how prayer should work. It's not like God doesn't know all of this stuff anyway. So take what He already knows about the good, the bad, and the ugly, and just sink it into a bath of prayer. Maybe that way, you can get it cleaned up!

In order to better understand how to do this, let me take this passage and suggest a few focal points for prayer.

Pray Always

First things first, pray! Pray early and pray often. Just never stop praying. Let me ask a question here. What point of your day does not need prayer? What part of your work does not need prayer? Which of your children do not need prayer? What part of your marriage does not need prayer? Truth be told, every moment of every day of our lives needs prayer. There are no exceptions. There really should be no prayer-free zones in our lives. Everything in our lives should be "bathed in prayer." This means that I should start praying when I get up in the morning, and then my day should be a constant conversation with the Holy Spirit who is going to see me through the entire day. That's how every day should go. Don't take these words as a guilt trip and feel bad because you didn't do enough or pray enough today. Take these words as an encouragement and seek out the focus in your own prayer life to start praying and keep praying.

Pray for Leaders

Now, allow me a stretch of the verse here. When the apostle asks the Colossians to pray for him, he is their pastor and the evangelist of his day. He also is their leader. They are going to find direction and instruction from him, and they are going to follow him. Some of them will follow him, in the name of Christ, to their deaths. We should constantly pray for those who lead us. At every level, there are people who are working to lead us onward and upward. Some of them are awesome at it and others are only mediocre. No matter what, they are our leaders. Leaders are often misunderstood. They are seen as always having the right answers, the right direction, or the right ideas. But that isn't always true. Leaders are, first and foremost, human. We have no superhuman leaders in our world. They are all just fallible human beings. We complain about them, vote for them, vote against them, yell at them, desire to meet them, listen to them, love them, and hate them. How about we pray for them?

Pray for Pastors

Pastors are leaders, but they are more. When you take the office of pastor in a congregation, especially in an American context, you are expected to be a leader, saint, monk, counselor, evangelist, rock star, businessman, politician, servant, and flawless family man. It's a big job! And no one can do it all. So, again, pray for your pastor. Pray *"that God may open a door for our message, so that we may proclaim the mystery of Christ."* Pray that God would make your pastor the person they should be, even if that won't ever make them the pastor you want!

Pray for Wisdom

Never fail to pray for yourself. It is not selfish to pray for yourself, especially if you are praying with the right attitude. Listen to what the apostle suggests and pray that you would *"make the most of every opportunity."* You should pray that *"your conversation be always full of grace, seasoned with salt, so that you may know how to answer everyone."* In other words, ask God to guide your feet into the opportunities that the Holy Spirit has in store for you. Ask God to give you the right words coming from the right heart, so that you can know how to talk to people. Ask God to allow those words to come out right, so that people can hear them properly and be affected by them in God's ways and not your ways. Ask God to give you grace at all times and in all things.

Pray to Give God Thanks

He made us.

He saved us.

He filled us with His Spirit.

He will see us through.

EPILOGUE

You may be wondering how it is that the last reading happened before the last verse of the epistle. The answer to this is simple. From Colossians 4:7 to the end of the letter, the apostle Paul gives us a list of greetings for folks around him. As you read through these last words from this letter to the church in Colossae, hear the heart of the man as he speaks of those who are his friends, helpers, supporters, and strength.

"Tychicus will tell you all the news about me. He is a dear brother, a faithful minister and fellow servant in the Lord. I am sending him to you for the express purpose that you may know about our circumstances and that he may encourage your hearts. He is coming with Onesimus, our faithful and dear brother, who is one of you. They will tell you everything that is happening here. My fellow prisoner Aristarchus sends you his greetings, as does Mark, the cousin of Barnabas. (You have received instructions about him; if he comes to you, welcome him.) Jesus, who is called Justus, also sends greetings. These are the only Jews among my co-workers for the kingdom of God, and they have proved a comfort to me. Epaphras, who is one of you and a servant of Christ Jesus, sends greetings. He is always wrestling in prayer for you, that you may stand firm in all the will of God, mature and fully assured. I vouch for him that he is working hard for you and for those at Laodicea and Hierapolis. Our dear friend

Luke, the doctor, and Demas send greetings. Give my greetings to the brothers and sisters at Laodicea, and to Nympha and the church in her house. After this letter has been read to you, see that it is also read in the church of the Laodiceans and that you in turn read the letter from Laodicea. Tell Archippus: 'See to it that you complete the ministry you have received in the Lord.' I, Paul, write this greeting in my own hand. Remember my chains. Grace be with you. "(Colossians 4:7-18)

From all of this, we should learn the art of expressed gratefulness. When people help us, we should be sure to thank them for their help. When they help us privately, the thanks should perhaps be private. When their help is public, our thanks should be public. What our thanks should not be is absent. We must express the gratefulness that God puts in our hearts for all those who come alongside us in this journey through life. Let people know the good they have done. Let them know that you noticed and have been made better by their help and service. Remind them, as the apostle does here, that this message is specifically from you. It is personal. It is real. It is *"in my own hand."* And from my heart, I pray for you all …

Grace be with you.

REFERENCES

McGee, J. Vernon. 1983. *Thru The Bible*. Nashville, Tennessee: Thomas Nelson Publishers.

Spence, H. D. M. and Joseph S. Exell. 1950. *The Pulpit Commentary*. Grand Rapids, Michigan: Wm. B. Eerdmans Publishing Company.

Strong, James. 2010. *The New Strong's Expanded Exhaustive Concordance of the Bible*. Nashville, Tennessee: Thomas Nelson Publishers.

The Heritage Foundation. 2017. *Family Structure and Children's Education*. http://www.familyfacts.org/briefs/35/family-structure-and-childrens-education.

Troutman, Katey. 2015. *Marriage Statistics: Are Americans Giving Up on Marriage?* http://www.cheatsheet.com/business/a-nation-of-singles-fewer-americans-are-married-than-ever-before.html/4/.

Marx, Karl and Friedrich Engels. 2016. *Manifesto of the Communist Party*. https://www.marxists.org/archive/marx/works/1848/communist-manifesto/.

All Scripture quotations are taken from the Holy Bible, New International Version.

ABOUT THE AUTHOR

Mike Hilson is the Senior Pastor of New Life Church based in La Plata, Maryland. Since 1999, the church has grown under his leadership from a congregation of less than 100 attendees into several churches and video venues. The New Life Network of churches now averages more than 5,000 in regular attendance across Maryland and Northern Virginia.

Mike currently serves on the Board of Trustees at Southern Wesleyan University. He also is a member of the Chesapeake District Board of Administration as well as the General Board of Administration of the Wesleyan Church. He lives in La Plata with his wife, Tina. They have three sons, Robert, Stephen, and Joshua, who have taken this journey of ministry with them.

Books by Mike Hilson include *Napkin Theology, Speak Life, A Significant Impact for Christ,* and a series of books called *Coffee with the Pastor.*